YOUR RIGHTS AT THE WORKPLACE

THE THINGS YOUR BOSS WON'T TELL YOU

Leo James Terrell
First edition

Leo Terrell Enterprises

Copyright © 1998 Leo Terrell Enterprises
All rights reserved: no part of this publication may be reproduced, stored in a retrieval system, or transmitted, in any form or by any means, electronic, mechanical, photocopying, recording, or otherwise, without the prior written permission of Leo Terrell Enterprises.

Manufactured in the United States of America
Library of Congress Catalog Card Number: 98-90603
ISBN: 0-9665828-0-2
Page design: James E. Knapp
Cover design: James E. Knapp

Publishers Cataloging-in-Publication Data

Terrell, Leo J.
    Your rights at the workplace: the things your boss won't tell you / by Leo James Terrell. -- 1st ed. p. cm

    1. Employee rights--United States. 2. Labor laws and legislation--United States. I. Title.

KF3319.3T47 1998	344.73'01
	QBI98-851

LEO TERRELL ENTERPRISES
8383 Wilshire Blvd #942
Beverly Hills, CA 90211
(213) 655-6805, fax (213) 655-5104
E-mail: leo@leoterrell.com
web site: http://www.leoterrell.com

CONTENTS

Dedication

Preface

Acknowledgements

About The Author

Introduction   xxiii

1 What Is Discrimination	27
2 The Employment Process	55
3 The Practice And Importance Of Documentation	69
4 Government Agencies Who Can Help You	83
5 Statute Of Limitations	91
6 The Litigation Process And How To Choose The Right Attorney	99
7 Summing It Up	113

Appendices:

A Contacting the EEOC	117
B Title VII Of The Civil Rights Act Of 1964	131
C Equal Pay Act Of 1963	185
D Age Discrimination In Employment Act	187
E Family And Medical Leave Act	219
F Americans With Disabilities Act	251

PREFACE

Being a civil rights attorney, I receive many calls of distress, pleas for help, and cries for relief every day. I have heard countless stories and examples of injustice, discrimination, hatred, harassment, and emotional assassination-the pain of which is only redoubled when the only thing I can say is "I'm sorry, but it's too late—nothing can be done." or "What evidence do you have to substantiate your assertions?" or even "...but you've signed away your right to sue..." I can't begin to tell you the frustration, anger, and impatience I feel when these injustices and injuries are tolerated and perpetuated—and only too slowly eradicated—all because people don't know their rights.

Empowering people to realize that they can determine the outcome of their lives, simply by knowing their rights, is not always easy. It would be far too tedious, exhausting, and time consuming to learn everything you need to know about the law...and that's where my practice in civil rights law and my experience as an educator come in.

In this book, I have summarized my knowledge and experience of civil rights law, case preparation, and courtroom procedure in a way that is straightforward and easily understood. I point out the snares, traps and pitfalls your employer can use to oppress and otherwise shatter your life at work. I explain your rights and privileges and guide you through the information you need in order to protect both yourself and your job.

I have striven to make this book clear and direct, by avoiding legalistic jargon, overbearing references, and excessive citations. My goal for this book is that it be an easy and helpful reference guide. In this book, you will learn to recognize infringements and unfair treatment which diminish your rights and happiness at work. You will know how to handle any situation that develops, and know what to do and where to go from there.

Relying on the axiom "Knowledge is power," my most ardent hope is that you will empower yourself with knowledge from this book. In so doing, you will become a force which repudiates injustice based on discriminatory acts. You will also help create a nation that honors its pledge of "liberty and justice for all."

ACKNOWLEDGEMENTS

    I would like to thank two of the most important people in my life: My mother, Isabella Terrell, and my father, Eddie Terrell, who recently passed away but is always present in my thoughts and heart. I dedicate this book to them because they have given me the foundation to be who I am today. I would be a liar if I said I have become who I am on my own. I am proud to have parents like my father and mother.

    I also want to thank Kristin Allen. Kristin and I have a love/hate relationship. Kristin made this project successful despite my own uneven temperament. She has been able to hang in there with me, and was chiefly responsible for helping me put this book together. No other person has made such a significant contribution to this book.

Finally, I want to thank all my clients. It has been through their cases that I can provide this information to you. Their turmoil, sadness and happiness have been the experiences I have relied on to create this project.

ABOUT THE AUTHOR

Leo James Terrell is a practicing civil rights attorney in Beverly Hills. In addition to the time he has devoted to building his solo practice, Mr. Terrell has served as head of the legal redress committee for the NAACP and co-chair of the Black-Korean Alliance. Because of his expertise, Mr. Terrell is frequently consulted by and appears on network television news programs, such as "Larry King", "Today Show", "Nightline" and "Good Morning America" as well as nationally syndicated radio programs like K.A.B.C. Newspapers, such as the Los Angeles Times and the Washington Post, have also interviewed and consulted with Mr. Terrell.

What makes Mr. Terrell unique is his thorough and energetic approach to his work. His style of presentation is influenced by his background in education. Prior to becoming an attorney, Mr. Terrell taught high school government and history and holds a M.A. degree in education. He is concerned not only in educating, but in captivating the interest of his audience- whether it be the courtroom, the lecture hall, or the on-camera debate. Mr. Terrell has that coveted gift of making things happen. His strength lies in his passion for doing right and inspiring that passion and motivation to act in others. The immediacy of his follow-through and his unceasing attention to detail are characteristic of Mr. Terrell and play significantly in the mix of his success.

For Mr. Terrell, the rewards of his successes are the resultant energy and enthusiasm with which he enters into his next pursuit. He is dedicated, hardworking and interested in your civil rights.

In his spare time, Mr. Terrell likes to work. His hobbies are work and working. His personal life centers around talking about work and/or strengthening business connections.

INTRODUCTION

The workplace is a major factor in people's lives. A full time employee, working forty hours a week, spends over two thousand hours a year at their job!!! However, these two thousand hours can turn into a nightmare in a job where you are a victim of discrimination, harassment or unfair treatment.

Unfortunately, many people do not understand that they have rights as an employee. They may not realize that the unpleasant, disturbing, annoying, provoking or frustrating conduct of the employer may be a form of discrimination that does not have to be tolerated. Many employees believe that the only solution to a hostile workplace is to either live with it or find another job. This is not the case. As an employee, you have the power to fight harassment and discrimination, and create a work environment that is free from this illegal conduct.

This book will help you learn exactly what discrimination is and what your rights are as an employee. It will demonstrate the difference between a work place that is illegal rather than just unpleasant. It will take you step by step to teach you how to handle work place discrimination and harassment, and how to make sure that you follow the proper procedures to protect your interests.

1 WHAT IS DISCRIMINATION?

Discrimination and harassment reveal themselves in many ways. They can be based on age, race, color, marital status, sexual orientation, physical or mental disability, or religion. The following examples are actual cases of discrimination committed by an employer:

I. When an employee was hired by a company, he clearly told them that he could not work on his Sabbath. When the workload at the company began to grow, the company had to continue production on eight Sundays a year. The employee refused to work on Sunday and was fired after four refusals.

II. A registered nurse with superior qualifications was denied a promotion in favor of another woman who was involved in an intimate relationship with the chief medical officer where she was employed.

III. A fifty-two year old employee was hired in 1977 and fired in 1986, a few weeks before his pension could vest, which caused him to lose his accrued benefits.

IV. A computer operator suffered from dyslexia. The company doctor recommended changes in the workplace, such as adjusting furniture to bring the computer screen closer to the operator's eyes and providing a different type of chair. The supervisor refused to make the modifications.

V. An African-American engineer was taunted by co-workers and supervisors with repeated racial comments, slurs and jokes, and shown cartoons displaying African-Americans in a negative fashion. Although the engineer repeatedly complained to management, management failed to take any corrective action.

VI. A waitress informed her employer that she was pregnant. When the waitress provided a note from her doctor saying that she was unable to "work until further notice", the employer said that he, and not her doctor, would decide whether or not she could work. The employer then fired the waitress because she "could not perform her duties."

VII. A Police Officer became H.I.V. positive and informed his employer that he needed to take two days off from work every month to receive medical treatment. After the second month, the employer refused to give the officer the requested time off. When the officer took the time off any way, he was fired.

VIII. A librarian of Asian (Indian) national origin was not reappointed for a second term because her employer said her "heavy accent and speech patterns prevented effective communication."

IX. An athletic gym employed male employees for its male facilities and female employees for its female facilities, however, they paid their male employees 7.5% of gross sales memberships to men and only paid their female employees 5% of gross sales memberships to females.

X. An employer required its female lobby attendant to wear a uniform which revealed her thighs and a portion of her buttocks. This uniform caused her to be subjected to numerous sexual propositions and comments from people walking through the lobby.

To help you understand what constitutes discrimination and harassment, we will now go over each of the categories and discuss them in detail.

A. UNFAIR TREATMENT • ADVERSE IMPACT

The most familiar form of discrimination is unfair or "disparate" treatment. Disparate treatment is when an employer treats an employee differently or less favorably because of their race, color, national origin, religion or sex. These types of cases usually involve a single employee complaining of an employer's intentional and discriminatory motive.

It is very important to remember that in order to prove discrimination, it must be shown that the employer treats the employee differently because of race, sex, or religion, etc. It is not necessarily discrimination if an employer "likes" someone better than you. It is not enough to be disciplined for the same thing that "Johnny" was not disciplined for, or to not get a raise when "Sue" got a raise. You must show that your employer did not give you the raise because you are a woman, or African American, or Jewish, etc. As you can imagine, therefore, proving a discriminatory motive is not always the easiest thing to do.

There are two ways to demonstrate discriminatory motive: direct evidence and circumstantial evidence. Direct evidence is the strongest form of proof.

For example, Texaco Oil settled a civil rights case for a huge sum because there were audio tapes showing managers and supervisors using racial slurs and derogatory references towards African-Americans. This was direct evidence and virtually indefensible.

Typically, though, you do not have such strong "smoking gun" evidence. In these situations, you rely on circumstantial evidence. Circumstantial evidence is the most common way to prove disparate treatment.

One of the most common examples of disparate treatment is when an employer fails to hire or promote an individual based on his/her race, color, national origin, religion, age or sex. In order to prove this type of case, an employee must show the following:

(1) That he/she is a member of a protected group (i.e. race, sex, religion etc.);
(2) That he/she applied and was qualified for the position;
(3) That he/she was rejected; and
(4) That the position remained open and the employer continued to seek applicants

If an employee establishes the above, the employer must then show a clear and reasonably specific nondiscriminatory reason for the employment decision. This may be demonstrated by showing that the individual eventually hired by the employer had more experience or skills, or by offering objective proof that the employee routinely behaved in an inappropriate way or had serious problems getting along with co-workers. The employer may not rely only on subjective opinions or simply state that they did what they thought was best.

The employee then has the chance to prove that the reasons given by the employer were not truthful and, in fact, were an excuse to hide the discrimination. The employee can accomplish this by either showing a court that the employer was more likely motivated by a discriminatory reason, or by showing that the reasons given by the employer for the action were unlikely or unbelievable.

The process described is similar to a tennis match: The employee has the ball and proves the four listed elements. If the employee is successful, then the ball is hit to the employer who shows that there was a good reason for the employment decision. If the employer is able to demonstrate a good reason, then the ball is hit back to the employee to show that the reason given is actually an excuse. If either side "drops the ball" and fails to demonstrate what they need to prove, then they lose.

Another related form of discrimination occurs when there is a "disparate impact." Disparate impact is where an employer has a hiring guideline or requirement which, on its face, appears to be neutral, but actually and disproportionately effects the members of a protected racial, sexual, religious or age group. Examples of guidelines which may result in a disparate impact are height and weight requirements, dress requirements, educational requirements, arrest and conviction records and drug history. Disparate impact is shown through statistics and does not require a discriminatory motive.

To invalidate a job requirement that has a disparate impact, the court again looks to a three step tennis match! First, using statistics, an employee demonstrates that the particular employment practice causes a disparate impact on a particular racial, sexual, religious or age group.

If the employee is successful, the employer must then prove that the requirement or selection guideline is actually related to the employee's ability to perform the job. For example, in a case claiming disparate impact, a court allowed a minimum height requirement for pilots which resulted in a significant percentage of women being disqualified. The evidence established that airplane cockpits are designed around a pilot's eye reference point. Therefore, if a pilot did not reach a certain height, their vision could be obstructed. The Court did rule, however, that the airline's requirement that a pilot be at least 5'7", which excluded 75% of female pilots but only 12% of male pilots, was not necessary for safety purposes, and therefore reduced the height requirement to 5'5", reducing the negative impact to female pilots.

If the employer successfully establishes that

the requirement or guideline is directly related to the employee's ability to perform the job, then the employee may still demonstrate that there were equal and alternate selection devices or criteria which served the employer's purpose but would not adversely impact any particular group.

The majority of discrimination cases involve issues of disparate treatment or disparate impact. Of the two, disparate treatment is the most difficult to establish, because you must prove that the intent or motive behind the treatment was to discriminate. Therefore, careful documentation is absolutely essential for employees who believe that they are being treated differently based on a discriminatory intent. Effective and proper documentation will be covered in detail in Chapter 3.

B. RELIGIOUS DISCRIMINATION

Employers are required to "accommodate" the religious observance, practices and beliefs of their employees, unless the employer can demonstrate that an accommodation would cause "undue hardship" on the employer's business.

In order to be eligible for an accommodation, an employee must sufficiently demonstrate that an employment requirement interferes with his/her own bona fide religious belief. The employee must show that the employer knew of the employee's religious belief, and nonetheless disciplined the employee for failing to obey the conflicting employment requirement.

Although possibly tempting, employees cannot simply state that they hold a belief which requires them to leave the office every Friday by 1:00 p.m. and come in no earlier that 11:00 a.m. on Monday, and then demand that the employer accommodate them!! Employees must first demonstrate that their belief is religious in nature. This is done by showing that their belief is based on a theory of "man's nature or his place in the Universe" which is sincere and not just a personal preference.

Once the employee establishes his/her legitimate religious belief, the employer is then required to reasonably accommodate the employee. This does not mean, however, that the employer has to provide the most reasonable accommodation.

For example, during the Vietnam war, two Postal Service window clerks stated that their religion opposed war, and therefore, their religious beliefs prevented them from processing draft forms. As an accommodation the employer transferred them to another position. The employees sued, saying that they should not be forced to transfer out of their current positions.

The court found that the employer's decision to transfer was a reasonable accommodation of the employee's beliefs, because it resolved the conflict and still maintained the clerks' employment status. However, the employer could not reduce or eliminate the employees' position or stature in their attempt to accommodate them.

An employer is not required to accommodate an employee if the employer can prove that every possible accommodation would cause an undue hardship to the business. An undue hardship is demonstrated by showing that the accommodation would impose on other coworkers, disrupt the routine at the workplace, or require the employer to bear more than a "de minimis" cost.

C. SEXUAL HARASSMENT

There are two types of sexual harassment. The first is a "quid pro quo" situation, where the employer or supervisor demands sexual favors in exchange for promotional opportunities or continued employment. The second situation occurs when a female employee is forced to endure a "hostile" or "abusive" work environment.

With "quid pro quo" discrimination, an employee must show that she experienced harassment because of sex, and that her reaction to the harassment had an actual effect on the terms and conditions of her employment. In other words, she must establish that her job, benefits or position depended on her acceptance of the sexual conduct.

There is also a related, yet different, "quid pro quo" situation involving a submission to sexual advances. When a qualified employee is denied a promotion or benefits in favor of another employee who has submitted to the sexual advances of a supervisor or owner, the employee being denied the opportunity is a victim of sex discrimination, even if the sexual requests were never directed towards her. Therefore, the stereotypical but age-old example of "sleeping their way to the top" may actually result in sex discrimination to the other, equally qualified employees in the office who are being denied the promotional opportunities.

The second form of sexual harassment arises out of a work place that is sexually hostile or abusive. In determining whether or not a workplace environment is hostile, the courts look to see whether a reasonable person would have found the environment to be hostile and whether or not the victim personally found the workplace to be sexually hostile. This means that the victim must show that most women would find the workplace environment to be offensive or harassing. The employer may not be responsible if the victim is particularly sensitive to certain issues, in comparison to the majority of women.

A sexually hostile environment can be created through both physical and verbal conduct. Examples of physical conduct are unwelcomed "massages" or "morning hugs", or the rubbing up against a woman. Equally offensive and inappropriate verbal harassment is demonstrated by the repeated use of derogatory and insulting terms relating to women, verbal abuse, sexual slurs and sexually provocative pictures. It is important to remember, however, that the conduct must be severe or prolonged. One isolated incident usually will not give rise to sexual harassment, as evidenced by a recent, highly political court case involving President Clinton and Paula Jones!

Frequently, in sexual harassment cases, and indeed in all types of discrimination cases, you must fight the stereotypes and prejudices of old school judges and jurors who refuse to acknowledge discrimination and harassment. It is possible to have a great case with strong evidence and get a bad judge or jury which will ruin your case.

Unfortunately, there are judges and juries who have personal agendas where they will ignore evidence because they refuse to accept the realities of life. In cases involving women, there are many who still follow the thinking of "she must have asked for it". In cases involving minorities, they may refuse to acknowledge that discrimination exists because they have never experienced it themselves.

In my years of practice as an attorney, I have tried many cases in front these types of people. While I will not name names because I don't want to get in trouble with the State Bar, I am sad to say that I have tried cases in front of judges who ignore the evidence. I have had juries that refuse to see what is clearly presented to them. Fortunately, with the steady increase of women in the workplace and many in positions of management and power, both sexes are gaining a sensitivity toward their co-employees, and are recognizing the importance of respect and courtesy in the workplace and at large. However, we still have a long way to go and we must fight against all forms of inappropriate behavior to ensure that it is never tolerated.

D. RACIAL HARASSMENT

Racial harassment is similar to a sexually hostile work environment. It may involve the use of racial slurs, demeaning racial graffiti, cartoons or literature, verbal threats and inappropriate racial jokes or references. Like sexual harassment, it is judged by a reasonable person standard, however, some people believe that this does not adequately take into account the pervasive existence of racism. They state that it fails to recognize the differences in which a minority would interpret a racial "joke" or slur as opposed to a non-minority.

In cases involving both racial and sexual harassment, you should be aware that managers and employers will attempt to downplay racial slurs and sexual innuendos as "playful jokes." Therefore, if you react in a positive way, or laugh at the "joke," it will be almost impossible to later complain about it. The bottom line is that you should not participate in, endorse, or laugh at conduct you find offensive. You need to let your employer know how you feel.

If an employee is being racially harassed by co-workers, the employee must show that the employer knew or should have known about the conduct and failed to do anything to correct the situation. The employer is responsible for taking reasonable steps to end the harassment.

E. RETALIATION

An employer is prohibited from retaliating against an employee who opposes the employer's conduct. For example, if the employee complains about an employer's discriminatory hiring practices, or supports someone else who complains, the employee cannot be subject to an adverse employment action, such as being fired.

CASE EXAMPLE:

A judge was terminated after his employer unlawfully received his medical records and decided that he was not medically fit to work. Two other judges opposed the termination, because they said it violated the Americans with Disabilities Act. The employer retaliated against the two judges by subjecting to unfair discipline, a hostile working environment and finally, termination.

In order to prove retaliation, an employee must show that:

(1) the employee opposed the employer's discriminatory conduct,
(2) the employer acted in a manner which had a

negative effect on the employee's job; and
(3) the employer acted solely because of the employee's opposition to the employer's discriminatory conduct.

Courts have typically made it easy to establish an employee's "opposition" of the employer's actions. The employee must demonstrate that he/she acted because he/she either:

(1) believed in good faith that the employer acted illegally or,
(2) had a reasonable basis for believing that the employer acted illegally.

Then, any action taken by the employee in response to his/her beliefs is strictly protected, and the employer is prohibited from retaliating against the employee for the action.

Employees are entitled to oppose all illegal conduct directed towards them, and are also protected if they oppose discrimination directed against other people. As demonstrated by the above example, the employer discriminated against the first judge by violating the Americans with Disability Act. The other two judges were not the initial targets of this illegal conduct. They voluntarily inserted themselves into the situation by fighting against the other judge's termination and stating that the employer's actions were illegal. Their behavior was absolutely protected.

Another case example involved two married clients of mine who worked at the same place. The wife filed a complaint of discrimination against her manager with the Equal Employment Opportunity Commission (EEOC). The husband testified on her behalf. After testifying, the husband was denied a promotion by the same manager who supervised the wife. This was illegal.

The purpose behind the law is to encourage people to stand up and fight against workplace discrimination and illegal conduct. The laws are therefore designed to protect people who oppose wrongdoing. Courts have said that these individuals may not be subjected to harassment or punishment as a result of their actions. They must be protected from retaliation by the employer.

The most frequent, example of retaliation occurs after the employee files a complaint or lawsuit against the employer. Once an employee has filed a complaint and/or lawsuit, any improper, biased or unlawful actions taken by the employer may be directly linked to the complaint, thereby creating a clear case of retaliation.

If the employee finds him/herself in a situation where he/she has filed a complaint and is subjected to retaliation by his/her employer, it is crucial that the employee document everything in order to support his/her case. Proper and effective methods of documentation will be discussed in detail in

Chapter Three.

F. AGE DISCRIMINATION

The "Age Discrimination in Employment Act of 1967" (ADEA) has become an increasingly effective tool to fight layoffs and discrimination of older workers. Now that the Baby Boomer generation is reaching forty and above, the question of older people's rights in the workplace has been brought to the forefront of civil rights litigation.

Generally, the Act states that employers may not discriminate against workers over the age of forty. Again, as in the previous discussion of disparate treatment, an employee's case usually focuses on the discriminatory motive of the employer. One of the most common examples of discriminatory motive is when an employer demotes or terminates an employee because of his/her age. In order to prove this type of case, an employee must show the following:

(1) That he/she is over forty years of age;
(2) That he/she was qualified, in that he/she had done satisfactory work;
(3) That he/she was discharged or demoted; and
(4) That he/she was replaced.

Generally the employee must be replaced with an individual who is not a member of the protected group (not over forty years of age). However, it may be sufficient to merely demonstrate that the individual who replaced the employee was younger. The case then gets stronger as the difference in ages increases.

If an employee establishes the above, as in disparate treatment, the employer must then show a clear and reasonably specific nondiscriminatory reason for the employment decision. This may be demonstrated by showing that the employee did not perform his/her job in a satisfactory manner, or that he/she had engaged in some type of misconduct on the job.

The employee then has the chance to prove that the reasons given by the employer were not truthful and, in fact, were an excuse to hide the discrimination. The employee can accomplish this by showing the court that age was a factor which made a difference in the employer's decision.

Again, as previously described, the process is similar to a tennis match: The employee has the ball and proves the four listed elements. If the employee is successful, then the ball is hit to the employer who shows that there was a good reason for the employment decision. If the employer is able to demonstrate a good reason, then the ball is hit back to the employee to show that the reason given is actually an excuse. If either side "drops the ball" and fails to demonstrate what they need to prove, then they lose.

G. DISABILITY DISCRIMINATION

The American with Disabilities Act of 1990 (ADA) protects employees with physical and mental impairments from discrimination in the workplace. One manner in which an employer can discriminate against an employee is by refusing to "reasonably accommodate" a disabled individual.

CASE EXAMPLE:
Casey Martin is a professional golfer with a leg injury that makes it difficult to walk the golf course. PGA rules require the player to walk the course, and prohibits the use of golf carts. Casey requested that he be permitted to use a golf cart because of his disability and the PGA refused. The court reversed the PGA, saying that Casey's need for a golf cart did not interfere with his ability to do his job (play golf!) and therefore the PGA had to reasonably accommodate him by allowing him to use the cart.

The above example, while extreme and unusual, demonstrates the commitment made by the Courts to individuals with disabilities. The American's with Disabilities Act of 1990 (ADA) defines a disability as a physical or mental impairment which substantially limits the ability of an individual to participate in a major life activity. In other words, if an individual is either completely unable to perform a major life activity, or is significantly restricted as to the manner or duration which he/she can perform the life activity, as compared to other average people, then he/she is considered disabled. "Major Life Activities" which are covered by the act include walking, breathing (lung disease), learning (mental retardation), and intimate sexual relations (H.I.V.). Some other unusual conditions which have been deemed as disabilities under the ADA are psychological disorders, alcoholism, sterility, and HIV disease. Some conditions which do not constitute a disability under the Act are environmental, cultural and economic disadvantages, homosexuality, and temporary impairments such as a broken leg.

The ADA forbids discrimination against qualified individuals with disabilities. In order to get relief under the ADA, an employee must show that:

(1) He/she is disabled within the meaning of the ADA,
(2) He/she is qualified, either with or without an accommodation, to perform the essential functions of the job, and
(3) the employer fired him/her or refused to hire him/her because of the disability.

One important feature of the ADA is that it requires an employer to "reasonably accommodate" a disabled employee. This means that the employer must make an attempt to adjust the employee's workplace conditions in order to assist the employee in performing his/her essential job functions. The employer is not required to make adjustments which would result in a change of the essential job functions of the position.

An example of an accommodation is the employer placing ramps or wider doorways at the workplace so an employee has easier access to the facility. An employer may also be required to eliminate certain non-essential job functions, delegate certain assignments to other employees, or re-design certain policies or procedures to allow the employee to perform the job responsibilities. An employer may be required to modify the employee's schedule or allow him/her to work part time. However, the employer is not required to make these accommodations if they would cause a hardship on the other employees at the job.

The key to reasonable accommodation is proving that the employee can perform all of the essential elements of the job, other than the few, non-essential elements which may be modified or eliminated through accommodations. The essential functions of the job are the "fundamental job duties." There are three factors used to determine whether or not something is a fundamental job function:

(1) whether the position is there for the purpose of performing that job function,
(2) whether there are a limited number of em-

ployees who the task can be delegated to, and (3) whether a replacement employee would be hired based on their ability to perform that particular function.

If the employer can show that the employee was unable to perform his/her fundamental job duties, the employer is not required to attempt to accommodate the disability.

The employer is also not required to make accommodations which would require significant expense or would be extremely disruptive or difficult. This is decided on a "case-by-case" basis. This means that the Court would take into consideration the size, income, and ability of the employer to make the accommodation. Additionally, the employer is not required to provide the accommodation if the employee can pay for the accommodation or obtain funding from another source.

The Americans with Disabilities Act has had a tremendous effect on workplace conditions and has brought the needs and abilities of the disabled to the country's attention. It has also provided the opportunity for hundreds of thousands of skilled and qualified individuals to prove their ability to contribute to the workplace. Disabled does not mean "unable."

H. FAMILY AND MEDICAL LEAVE ACT

Another provision prohibiting workplace discrimination, harassment and unfair treatment is the Family and Medical Leave Act of 1993. (FMLA). The Family and Medical Leave Act applies to any employer who employs 50 or more employees for over 20 weeks a year. In order to benefit from the Act, the employee must demonstrate:

1. The employee has worked for the employer for over 12 months;
2. The employee has worked at least 1,250 hours during the last 12 months; and
3. The employer has fifty or more employees working at the worksite of the employee requesting the leave.

If the employee qualifies under the Act, the employee is entitled to receive up to 12 weeks of unpaid leave per year for the birth or adoption of a child, to care for a parent, child or spouse with a serious health problem, or if the employee is unable to perform the functions of his/her job due to a serious health condition. The leave may be taken as one long block of time or be limited to the needs of the employee, such as two hours twice a week for chemotherapy.

Under these circumstances, the employer can neither terminate the employee nor can they discontinue the employee's health insurance coverage. The employee, however, is still responsible for paying the regular insurance premiums or employee contribution. After the leave has ended, the employer must rehire the employee to the same or substantially similar job position. This means that the employee is entitled to return to the identical or equivalent job with the equivalent pay, benefits, terms and conditions such as schedule, work location, and opportunity for bonuses. If an employee requests time off under the Act, the employer is responsible for explaining the employee's responsibilities and obligations.

Unfortunately, since the Family Medical Leave Act is fairly recent, many employees do not know their rights and responsibilities under the Act. They do not realize that they do not have to choose between their job and the loving and devoted care of a parent, child or spouse. They also do not realize that their own illness cannot be an excuse for termination.

I. EQUAL PAY ACT

The Equal Pay Act prohibits an employer from basing an employees' salary on their sex. In other words, equal work deserves equal pay, regardless of whether the employee is a man or woman. There are only four exceptions to the rule:

(1) The pay is based on a seniority system;
(2) The pay is based on a merit system;
(3) The pay is based on a system which measures earnings by quantity or quality of production;

or

(4) The pay is based on some factor other than sex;

In order for an employee to show a violation of the Equal Pay Act, he/she must show that two employees of the opposite sex are receiving unequal pay because of their sex. The two employees' jobs must require equal skill, effort and responsibility and be performed under similar working conditions.

It is generally easier to demonstrate a case of unfair wages when the job involves a fixed, hourly rate of pay and involves unskilled and semiskilled labor. When the position involves more skill and training it may require irregular hours, so it is more difficult to compare.

If an employee can demonstrate a violation of the Equal Pay Act, the employer is required to raise the salary of the lower paid employee. The employer cannot reduce the wage of the higher paid employee. The employer can also be responsible for back wages, which is the amount of money the employee would have received if he/she had been paid fairly. For example, if Thomas received ten dollars per hour for the past year and Cindy only received eight dollars per hour for the last year, Cindy may be entitled to a lump sum payment of an additional two dollars for every hour she worked in the past year.

CASE EXAMPLE:
A health club alternated on a daily basis between being a health club for men and a health club for women. Therefore, on Monday, Wednesday and Friday, the club was for women and only employed female workers for those days. On Tuesday, Thursday and Saturday, the club was exclusively for men, with male workers. The male employees received 7.5% of all membership sales while the female workers received 5% of all sales. Although the women overall made the same amount of money as the men, since more women signed up annually, the Court still held that the percentages violated the Equal Pay Act since they were based solely on gender.

2 THE EMPLOYMENT PROCESS

So, how do you avoid being put in a situation where you are treated unfairly at work? Through knowledge of the employment process, you will have the ability to greatly reduce the possibility of having problems at work. Knowing your rights from the moment you begin your employment will help your sense of personal security in the workplace.

Many times, when people start a new job they are slightly intimidated and do not want to "rock the boat", so they do not find out what they can expect as an employee of the company. There are six questions that employees should ask their employer:

(1) Is there an Employee Handbook or Collective

Bargaining Agreement?
(2) What type and length of training will I receive?
(3) How are employees advised of promotional opportunities?
(4) What grievance procedures are available to employees?
(5) Will I be required to sign a waiver of my rights?
(6) What are my rights as an "at-will" employee?

Many employees will begin a job not knowing the answers to these questions. This is very dangerous. If you do not know what the objective job guidelines are, or if there are no objective guidelines, it will be very difficult to demonstrate if you are being treated unfairly. Therefore, we will address each of the six categories separately.

A. EMPLOYEE HANDBOOK • COLLECTIVE BARGAINING AGREEMENT

An employee handbook is typically prepared by the employer. A collective bargaining agreement is negotiated between the union and the employer. Both lay out the terms and conditions of employment. They specify the rights and responsibilities of both the employee and employer. Among other things, the employee handbook or collective bargaining agreement should contain sections relating to the grievance procedure, promotions and training for the employee, and an anti-discrimination clause. Since these sections are crucial, we will also discuss them individually.

Why, do you ask, is an employee handbook or collective bargaining agreement important? Well, imagine a workplace without any rules or guidelines. The employer then has complete discretion to decide if something does or does not violate the workplace policy. All of a sudden, you could be written up for "smiling on a Friday." "But," you cry, "I smiled last Friday and didn't have a problem!" "Ah Hah!!" Your employer states. "But last Friday was the 13th, and it was o.k. to smile. Today, being the 20th, is an absolute violation."

Obviously, the above example is ridiculous. However, it does demonstrate the absolute control an employer has if there is no employment agreement. There is no objectivity and the employer has total discretion to decide whether or not an employee is following the terms and conditions of his/her employment. While this does not mean that employers can get away with whatever they want, it does give them a better opportunity to justify their conduct.

If you have an employee handbook, you know what is expected of you and you know what you can and cannot do. You know what will happen to you if you do not follow the employee handbook. If your employer does not follow the agreement, it allows you to objectively demonstrate his unfair treatment.

All large companies should have an employee handbook. Typically, the handbook is kept in the Human Resources Department. If you do not have a Human Resources Department, you may ask your manager or supervisor for a copy. You may also go to your union representative if there is one.

If your employer is a large company and does not have an employee handbook, you should seriously question its absence. You need to ask yourself if you should be working for a company that does not have objective guidelines for its employees. It is highly irregular and may be a warning sign of possible future problems.

Not every employer has an employee handbook. Frequently, small businesses will not have an handbook. However, this does not prevent you from suggesting that you and your employer agree on what each expects from the other. If done properly, your employer should be impressed at your initiative and sense of responsibility. Obviously, the suggestion should be done in a professional and courteous manner. It should not suggest that you anticipate any problems. You may simply state that it would be helpful to clearly understand your rights and responsibilities, therefore you would like to discuss and write down the terms and conditions of employment.

Even if you are hired in the position of a manager, you should ask your employer if there is such a thing as a Manager's Handbook. As a manager, you also have rights and responsibilities, so it is also safer and easier for you if they are carefully spelled out in writing.

Finally, the saying "an ounce of prevention is worth a pound of cure" is directly applicable to the workplace. The more you know about your rights and responsibilities, and the more your employer knows that you are aware, the less likely it is that you will have problems. And if you do have problems, they will be much easier to demonstrate and document.

B. TRAINING AND EVALUATIONS

In order to be an effective and efficient employee, you are entitled to some form of job training. It is rare for you to be expected to show up on your first day of work and jump right in, without any orientation or demonstration of your duties.

Your employer should already have a training program established when you start. If not, you should ask your employer to assign you to someone in your job classification so that you can follow them and observe for a period of time. The amount of time necessary for observation will vary from job to job, but it is a very important feature. By observing other employees, you are able to gain first-hand knowledge of how they are performing their job duties. Typically, the employer will assign you to train with someone who the employer believes is an outstanding, or at least, satisfactory, employee. By observing this individual, you will have a good opportunity to see how the employer wants the job done.

The ideal work situation allows you to observe a fellow employee in the performance of his/her duties, and then provides you with the opportunity to perform the job under the guidance of your trainer. If your employer does not have a specific training program, you should request this type of training. At the end of the training, it is best if there is an evaluation which specifies each of your job responsibilities and then confirms that you were able to successfully perform each function. This way, there is a clear record of your training and abilities—and everyone knows what you have or have not been trained to do.

Ideally, your employer should also provide you with regular performance evaluations throughout your employment. This allows another objective history of your performance with the company, and it also gives you written confirmation of your job duties and responsibilities. If your employer does not automatically provide written evaluations, consider requesting one on an annual or bi-annual basis.

Evaluations may also contradict unfair treatment by your employer. For example, I represented a woman who was the Assistant Superintendent of a school district. She was called to testify at an EEOC hearing regarding a third party complaint, and she testified honestly that she had warned the school board about some suspicious discriminatory hiring practices. Less than a week after she testified, the school board notified her that it would not renew her contract, and that she was being terminated "for good cause." Fortunately, however, since my client had a documented history of excellence, I was easily able to accurately contradict the false charges of dismissal.

C. PROMOTIONS

One thing that is important to know when you begin a new job is the opportunities available for advancement. Are promotional opportunities posted in advance and open to all qualified employees? Are promotional opportunities based on objective qualifications, such as seniority or a written exam?

If an employer does not post all job opportunities or does not utilize neutral or objective hiring criteria, there is a greater possibility that the hiring practices may have a disparate impact or involve disparate treatment, as previously discussed in Chapter One. This is because the employer only opens up job positions to those individuals they want to hire, thereby excluding all others from consideration.

Employees may challenge promotional decisions if they have a disparate impact or involve disparate treatment. Employment decisions may also be challenged if employers improperly fail to publicize the opening or have policies and/or procedures which discourage individuals in a given protected group (i.e. age, sex, race, etc.) from applying for the position.

The best way for an employer to list employment and promotional opportunities is to provide a written announcement of the position and publicize it in a way that allows all employees to receive notice of the opening. In addition, whenever possible, the employer should use objective qualifications to base their employment decision. Obviously this is not always possible, however, the courts have generally been more understanding of subjective requirements when the position is management or a professional position, rather than a job requiring little skill or experience. If the employer is going to use subjective criteria in the employment decision, the employer should clearly identify the essential requirements of the job and specify what qualities the employer is looking for in an applicant.

D. GRIEVANCE PROCEDURE

One of the most important things to know about your job is the grievance procedures available to you if you have a problem. These should be thoroughly described in your employee handbook. If not, or if you do not have an employee handbook, you should find out the proper channels to go to for any problems you may have.

If your employer does not have specific grievance procedures, you should take any problems you have to your immediate supervisor. Always make sure that you are discussing problems with someone who has the ability to change the situation. Simply complaining to co-workers is insufficient to protect your rights.

If your employer or supervisor is not helpful or responsive to your problems and you have no internal assistance, you may need to go outside of the workplace to find a solution. In this case, you could either go to the Equal Employment Opportunity Commission (EEOC), or the Office of Federal Contract Compliance (OFCC). These entities are important parts to any claim of employment discrimination or unfair treatment. They are discussed in greater detail in Chapter Four.

E. EMPLOYEE WAIVERS

If you are about to start a new job, beware of your employer's attempt to get you to sign a waiver. A waiver limits an employee's rights. It generally states that you will not take the employer to court if they discriminate against you. Your only available option is to pursue the matter in arbitration.

Arbitration is a process where you present your evidence of discrimination to an arbitrator. The arbitrator may be an attorney or retired judge. The arbitrator then decides the case and you are bound by the decision. You are not entitled to a jury trial and typically an arbitrator's award, if any, is very modest. This is because the arbitrator wants to be hired again by the employer in the future, so he does not want any controversial rulings.

Most types of employee waivers are illegal, however, it may be a long and hard road to fight. If you are offered a job and then asked by your employer to sign a waiver, it puts you in an understandably difficult position. It may be a violation to force you to sign the waiver, but if you don't, you may not get the job. If you are in this situation, you should ask your employer why you are being forced to sign the waiver and lose your rights.

Ultimately, you will have to decide whether or not you will sign the agreement. However, it is important for you to make this decision understanding the potentially serious consequences if you later have problems at work.

Another growing employer's trick is to tie a waiver to a severance package. The employee receives the benefits of the severance package as long as the employee agrees not to sue the employer for wrongful termination or age discrimination. Again, most of these types of waivers are illegal. If all employees are entitled to a severance package then the severance package is independent of any waiver agreement. The employer cannot condition the benefits on the waiver of rights.

Fortunately, unlike an employee that is asked to sign a waiver before they get the job, if you already have the job you are in a better position to refuse. Still, the employer knows that financial security is a powerful incentive. If you do not sign the waiver, your employer might refuse to provide you with an appropriate severance package. To protect older employees against improper waivers, the law generally requires an employer to permit a minimum of seven days for the employee to reconsider after signing the waiver.

Although you can fight back against illegal waivers, the court system is a long and difficult process. Your employer is counting on the likelihood that you cannot afford to wait to get what you deserve. Unfortunately, this is how the system has failed "the little guy."

For example, one of my clients was fired because she complained about clearly documented instances of racial discrimination. She hired me and we fought a long and hard battle through the courts. During this time, my sixty three year old client did not have any income. Although she saved wisely for retirement, she had been counting on her pension and retirement benefits from her employer. Since she was fired, she did not receive either. My client was forced to sell her house and she began to have serious financial difficulties. I believe that the employer knew they were going to ultimately lose, but they kept fighting and hoping that they could wear her down to where she would be desperate for money.

My client finally won a substantial amount from her employer, but it was an extremely difficult road with no guarantee of success.

Unfortunately, these are some of the realistic considerations you must evaluate before you decide to take on your employer. Fortunately, my client was an incredibly strong woman of character and she deeply believed that she had to stand up for what was right, regardless of the outcome. This is a tremendous decision and only you can decide what is right for you. What is important, is that you make your decision knowing all the facts.

F. AT-WILL EMPLOYMENT

Finally, I want to clear up any confusion about the term "at-will employment." This is another employer's trick which is frequently used.

At-will employment means that you do not have a guaranteed right to a job. Your employer may come in on Monday and say "Things are tight at work so I'm letting you go. You have two weeks." Or, your employer may say "My friend's nephew is taking over your position. You're out."

Unfortunately, although you may not like it, your employer does have the right to terminate you under these circumstances if your position is "at-will." However, at-will employment does not prevent an employee from complaining of harassment or discrimination, and if the employee is fired for these complaints, the employee may have a lawsuit for retaliation. In addition, you may not be fired from an at-will position because of your race, color, sex, national origin, disability or age. At-will employment may not guarantee you a right to a lifetime job, however, you are still guaranteed the right to be free from discrimination and harassment.

There is one important thing to remember when you fill out an at-will job application: Everything you write down must be the truth. Why? Because even if you have worked at a company for five or ten years, if you file a complaint of discrimination or harassment, the first thing your employer will do is pull your application to see if you had lied at all. If you had, the employer will say "You should not have been hired in the first place. You lied." The information on the application may be totally unrelated to your job performance or abilities, but your employer will try to use it against you to discredit you.

When you fill out an employment application, do not be sloppy. Do not guess about the information you are giving the employer. It could come back to haunt you.

3 THE PRACTICE AND IMPORTANCE OF DOCUMENTATION

In my years of experience as a civil rights and employment attorney, I have talked to thousands of people who were experiencing problems at work. Sometimes, the problems described were only the unfortunate result of an unpleasant work environment. I would repeatedly explain to these people that employers do not have to be nice or pleasant. They just have to be fair. And they don't always have to be fair, either. There is nothing illegal about an employer treating one employee better than another, or letting another employee do things that they will not allow you to do. An employer can act or treat their employees differently unless they are treating the employee differently because of their race, sex, age, gender, national origin, disability, etc.

Unfortunately, however, many of the calls I received were legitimate and often outrageous examples of harassment, retaliation and discrimination. As previously mentioned, they included an Assistant Superintendent of a School District who was fired for testifying at a Federal Equal Employment Opportunities Commission hearing regarding illegal hiring practices. A Police Officer fired for taking time off from work for medical treatment after being diagnosed with the H.I.V. virus. An African-American engineer forced to endure constant racial taunts, derogatory slurs and names, and racially offensive jokes and cartoons directed towards him by co-workers and management. A female secretary repeatedly threatened with the loss of her job unless she acted "a little nicer" towards the boss and agreed to go out with him.

These cases were all real and shocking examples of outrageous abuse by the employer. These employees came to me out of desperation, hoping that I would be able to provide some relief or answers for them. For many people, I was able to help them. Others, however, had no chance. They may have failed to take action soon enough and the statute of limitations had set in, or they had failed to follow the internal administrative requirements. These two situations can automatically nullify any claim—regardless of how legitimate or outrageous.

The employee may have also failed to keep written documentation which recorded the employer's actions, detailed the history of the behavior, and demonstrated the employer's failure to take corrective action. Without this information, it becomes your word against your employer. Even if you think you have "witnesses", they are frequently co-workers who will not testify on your behalf for fear of jeopardizing their own jobs. This is the sad but unfortunate reality of employment cases. Most of my clients have said "I have at least a dozen witnesses." This makes me smile, shake my head, and think "stop kidding yourself." No one is going to lose their job to save yours. Some of these people are pawns of management who are wiling to sacrifice you for their own career advantage.

I had one case that involved a police organization who was using the polygraph examination as an excuse to disqualify African-American applicants. This case was extremely political and vigorously fought. And for the first time in my years of practicing law, I had a longstanding employee testify against his employer on behalf of my client.

The employee admitted that the individual in charge of the employment unit had said that "black applicants needed to be scrutinized more carefully because of their inherent violent nature." This testimony was devastating to the employer and I was stunned at his honesty. You ordinarily do not find employees risking their job for someone else.

Proper and effective documentation is the only real method for showing a clear and authentic picture of harassment and discrimination at work. Without proper documentation, you may jeopardize your position and your case.

WHAT TO DOCUMENT

In Chapter One of this book, I identified many different forms of workplace harassment and illegal conduct. If you believe that you are the victim of one of these forms of unfair treatment, it is important for you to document what is happening at work.

In every situation involving workplace issues, the courts require the employee to inform the employer of any problems, thereby putting the employer on "notice" of the illegal conduct. In other words, this means you must tell your employer what you believe to be the unfair or inappropriate treatment, and give them an opportunity to correct the situation. If you do not take this step, the first defense taken by the employer will be, "He/she never told me. I would have fixed the problem immediately if I would have only known." Whether this is true or not, you will lose your case if you do not have any proof that you had made your employer aware of the problem and they refused to correct it.

Certain claims of discrimination or employee's rights require the employee to notify his/her employer of the special circumstances before or immediately after they happen. For example, in a claim of religious discrimination, one of the three elements an employee must prove is notice to employer. Additionally, he/she must show that:

(1) The employee has a bona fide religious belief that conflicts with an employment requirement;
(2) The employee informed the employer of this belief; and
(3) The employee was disciplined for failure to comply with the conflicting employment requirement

If the employer did not know about the religious conflict, they had no obligation to accommodate the employee.

Similar situations arise in cases involving the Family Medical Leave Act and the Americans with Disabilities Act. If the employee does not tell his/her employer that they are experiencing serious difficulties at home caring for a child, parent or spouse, and simply takes off excessive amounts of time, the employee runs the risk of being terminated. Along the same line, an employer cannot be expected to accommodate an employee with a disability unless the employer knows the limitations and difficulties the employee is experiencing.

So, the first step is to put your employer on notice of the problem. Make them aware of what is happening to you. AND DO IT IN WRITING. There is no stronger evidence than documents which support your position. This is commonly referred to as the "paper trail." If done properly, a paper trail can lead your way out of a problem just like Hanzel & Gretel's bread crumbs. It also locks your employer into his/ her actions by not allowing your employer to change history and invent a different story or sequence of events.

Proper documentation may also guarantee that co-workers or witnesses will not change their story. If you are in a situation where you have co-workers as witnesses, ask them to write a statement regarding what they observed. Then give copies of these statements to management. Do not keep them secret. Let management have a clear picture of the problems you are having.

When you notify your employer of the problems you are experiencing, make sure you date the letters, make it specific and non-threatening and REQUIRE A RESPONSE. For example:

> Dear Mr. Smith, On January 1, 1998, I was approached by Mr. Johnson in the hallway. Mr. Johnson kept touching me on the arms and back even though I attempted to move away from him. When I asked him to please stop and move out of my way, he became angry and accused me of being "cold and unfriendly." Please speak to Mr. Johnson regarding this situation and respond to this letter within two weeks. Sincerely, Sue Williams.

This letter accomplishes three purposes. The first thing it does is to call attention to the problem. It is a serious matter which needs to be investigated. Secondly, by putting the complaint in writing, the employer knows that you are serious and committed to your position. It is less likely that they will ignore your problem because they know that you have made the situation "official" by properly documenting your complaint and requesting a response. Your employer is more likely to respond because they will be well aware of the consequences if they fail to act.

If the employer does not respond to your first letter, what should you do? Write another letter. Refer again to the date of your first letter and say "You have failed to respond to my letter dated January 1, 1998, regarding my difficulty with Mr. Johnson. I had requested that you respond by January 14, 1998. As of this date, I have not received a reply. Please respond to this situation by February 15, 1998."

I cannot stress the importance of proper documentation. It is generally the one thing that will ensure the success or failure of your case.

Many prospective clients have said that they did not document anything or advise their supervisors of the problem because they were scared of what would happen. They also said that their problem actually involved the people they would complain to, so they thought it would only make things worse.

What I try to explain is that the documentation

gives you power, because not only have you placed these people on notice of the problem, but you have protected yourself against possible retaliation. If your employer retaliates against you or harasses you based on your complaint, you have your original complaint to back you up plus the new complaint which you will write for retaliation. In addition, if your employer retaliates against you for complaining, it, in effect, confirms the original complaint.

WHO TO SUBMIT THE DOCUMENT TO

Documentation is important because it puts your employer on notice of the problem and also protects your position in case the problem persists. In order to properly place your employer on notice, you need to present your written complaint to a Supervisor or Manager or someone in the company with authority to correct the situation. It is not enough to tell other employees or even the co-worker that is causing the problems. You must tell someone who can put an end to the situation.

The best person to give your grievance to is your immediate supervisor. He/she then has the responsibility to either take action, or make sure that someone higher up acts appropriately. You do not have the responsibility to take your complaints to the highest authority in the company. You have the right to assume that corrective action will be taken if you properly inform your immediate supervisor.

What if your immediate supervisor is the person

you are having problems with? Then give your written complaint to the person who supervises your supervisor, or the Human Resources Department. The key is to make sure you give it to someone who can help you. Saying, "I can't give it to them because they are the bad guys" is the worst thing to do in the situation. It basically guarantees that you will never receive the help you need.

HOW TO DOCUMENT

The key to good documentation is to have everything in writing and keep copies for yourself. After documenting the troublesome situation for the first time and presenting your supervisor with a copy (keeping an extra copy for yourself), you should continue to keep a journal of any more improper activity. You may simply keep a notebook and note the day, time, and individuals involved, and write a brief description of what happened. Be as detailed as possible and try to remember any spoken words as accurately as possible. If the conduct at work continues, and you find you must keep an ongoing journal, make sure that you do not leave the journal at work at any time. It should remain in your personal possession at all times, in a briefcase or purse.

Any additional incidents should be documented in writing and you should continue to attempt to solve the problem by notifying your employer of the continued difficulties. Again, this should always be done in writing, and your supervisor should always be asked to provide a response to your complaint.

Make sure that you document according to the guidelines of the employee handbook or your employer's grievance procedure. Be aware of any requirements or guidelines for submitting complaints. Ask your supervisor or the Human Resources Manager, or look in your employee handbook to find the proper procedure. This is very important. If the handbook says that you should submit all complaints to the Manager, then submitting a letter to the President will not be very effective.

If your employer continues to refuse to take any action on your behalf, or if the action taken is inadequate, you may have to ultimately seek relief in another manner, perhaps by filing a charge with the EEOC. However, you should make sure that you have first given your employer clear notice of the problems and given them every opportunity to correct the situation. If your case goes to trial and you have properly documented all the problems and can demonstrate that you tried to get help but management did not respond, you have an excellent chance of winning.

Do not believe an employer who tells you not to document your problems. They may say, "We can handle this informally" but do not be deceived. An employer knows exactly how good documentation may be used against them in court. Therefore, the employer tries to keep you from putting things in writing so they can minimize any proof of your complaints. Then, if necessary, they can make up their own version of events and you have nothing in writing to contradict them.

What if your employer responds to your letter and sets up a meeting with you? These meetings are generally stacked against the employee. They have four or five managers and company people against just you, so try to even out the situation. Ask to record the meeting so you can have an accurate record of what was said. I guarantee you most employers will not allow this, but if a company has nothing to hide, they should not have a problem.

If you cannot record the meeting, ask if you can take notes. Why is this important? Well, I guarantee that your employer will have someone present taking notes and documenting the meeting. However, this person will be taking notes based on the employer's point of view. This may be biased and not entirely accurate. By taking your own notes, you have a more balanced record of what happened.

You should also ask if you may have a representative at the meeting. Then get a trusted friend or advisor to sit in with you. If you are in a union, you can ask to have your union representative present but BEWARE of unknown union representatives. Although I am a union supporter, I have unfortunately seen many situations where the union does not represent the employee's best interests. Make sure someone you trust is present.

HOW MUCH IS TOO MUCH?

This is a difficult section to explain. Sometimes a legitimate claim of inappropriate behavior, discrimination, retaliation or harassment may become buried in a sea of irrelevant, suspicious fear. In other words, if an employee claims that everything that ever happened to them is the result of some form of improper behavior by the employer, then truly wrongful conduct may be overlooked because of skepticism and a lack of concern.

This does not mean that an employee should tolerate unfair treatment by the employer. It simply reminds everyone of the story of the "Boy Who Cried Wolf." Right or wrong, an employer will use a history of false accusations as a defense against legitimate ones. I had a case where a client had ten spiral notebooks full of "documentation." Contained in these notebooks were about four pages that demonstrated serious abuses by the employer. However, the other 996 pages attempted to document how the supervisor "suspiciously and abruptly" asked where the employee had been when they weren't at their desk, or how the employee was required to correct a mistake in a report that, in the employee's words "wasn't a big deal." Unfortunately, by repeatedly complaining about things that were not unlawful or wrong, the employee created an impression that she was just a "complainer", and the employer's actual misconduct was lessened. Her own diaries were used against her by her employer at trial.

The best form of written documentation is the written complaints you give your supervisor. You cannot overdocument legitimate complaints. It is the best form of evidence.

4 GOVERNMENT AGENCIES WHO CAN HELP YOU

A. EQUAL EMPLOYMENT OPPORTUNITY COMMISSION

The EEOC came into being through Title VII of the Civil Rights Act of 1964. Its purpose is to enforce the principal federal statutes prohibiting employment discrimination. Some examples of applicable statutes are:

1. Title VII of the Civil Rights Act of 1964, which prohibits employment discrimination on the basis of race, color, religion, sex, or national origin;

2. Age Discrimination in Employment Act of 1967, which prohibits employment discrimination against individuals 40 years of age and older;
3. Equal Pay Act of 1963, which prohibits discrimination on the basis of gender in compensation for substantially similar work under similar conditions;
4. Title I of the Americans with Disabilities Act of 1990, which prohibits employment discrimination on the basis of disability in both the public and private sector; and
5. Section 501 of the Rehabilitation Act of 1973, which prohibits employment discrimination against federal employees with disabilities

If you believe that your employer is treating you unfairly or violating one of the above statutes, you may file a complaint, or "charge" with the EEOC. There are very strict deadlines for filing the charge. It must be filed within 180 days of the alleged discriminatory act. If the charge is not filed in a timely manner, you may lose your opportunity to seek relief through the court system. Since deadlines and statutes of limitations are critical to preserving your rights, we will discuss this topic separately and in greater detail in Chapter Five.

The EEOC has field offices throughout the United States. The offices investigate all charges to determine if there is "reasonable cause" that an employer has been discriminating against an employee. If the EEOC finds such "cause", it attempts to mediate to correct the problem. If the EEOC is not able to resolve the situation, the employee receives a "right to sue" letter and may then file a private lawsuit. The EEOC may also file a federal lawsuit against an employer for workplace discrimination and statutory violations.

The EEOC can be extremely helpful to your case or it may simply serve as an administrative hurdle which you must follow. For example, I have had several cases which were thoroughly investigated by the EEOC. One case, which I have previously mentioned, involved an Assistant Superintendent of a School District who was retaliated against after she testified against her employer at an EEOC hearing. Five days after her testimony, the employer gave her notice that her contract was not being renewed. As soon as she received notice, my client filed a charge of retaliation with the EEOC. The EEOC reviewed the matter, noticed that the nonrenewal of her contract occurred within days of her testimony, and immediately sent a letter to the school district advising it that the EEOC would not tolerate retaliation against employees who testified.

The EEOC did an extremely thorough investigation, and demanded that the school district provide responses to its inquiry. Since the EEOC is an independent federal agency, the employer knew that if they did not respond to the EEOC's inquiry, things would only get worse.

This case was the exception, however, because the EEOC does not have the time or resources to complete an in-depth investigation on all charges submitted to it. Instead, they usually process the claim and issue a "right to sue letter."

If the EEOC does an independent investigation, it can be extremely helpful if you go to trial. You are entitled receive a copy of your EEOC file, which will contain your employer's responses to the EEOC investigation. If you have done a good job of documenting your situation, any response the company gave you can be compared to the response they gave to the EEOC to see if they are consistent.

A very important point to remember regarding the EEOC is that every time there is a new incident, you must file a new charge. For example, I had a case where my client worked for a large aerospace company. She filed a complaint with the EEOC in 1989 regarding the company's failure to properly promote her. The EEOC did an independent investigation and found that her complaint was correct.

The EEOC settled the investigation by having the employer agree to promote my client. For four years my client waited for her promotion. Time after time, a promotional opportunity would come up and my client would not be promoted. Her employer would promise that they were "handling" the situation and that she would be promoted as agreed upon with the EEOC. They told her not to worry.

Finally, after years of waiting, my client went back to the EEOC to ask them to force the employer to abide by the agreement. Unfortunately, there was nothing the EEOC could do. The statute of limitations, which is the time deadline to bring a complaint, had already passed.

What my client should have done was to file another charge immediately after she lost the first opportunity to be promoted. Then, every time a promotion came up which was not given to my client, she should have filed another charge. This would have kept everything alive so the EEOC could enforce the agreement.

Every time there is a new incident, you need to file a new charge. If you are having problems with sexual harassment and you file a charge with the EEOC on January 1, 1998, and on February 14, 1998 you have another problem and your employer does not help you, go back to the EEOC. Why? Because if you end up having to go to trial, every incident is looked at separately. You may only go to trial on the incidents which have been properly brought to the EEOC's attention. You cannot lump everything together. You must follow the proper procedure for each and every occurrence. This means filing a charge with the EEOC for every situation.

For your convenience, a complete list of EEOC headquarters and field offices is provided in the index of this book.

B. STATE AGENCIES

The EEOC is a federal agency, which means that it applies nationally to every state. Some states, however, have their own state equivalent to the EEOC. The state agency is usually described as some form of "Fair Employment" agency. Forty six states, including Washington D.C., Puerto Rico and the Virgin Islands all have a "local" agency in addition to the EEOC. As of June, 1998, Alabama, Arkansas, Louisiana and Mississippi do not have a state agency.

Since this book covers national guidelines, which apply to everyone, we will not discuss the individual state agencies. It is only important for you to know that they exist, and you may be referred to these agencies by the EEOC if it is appropriate.

5 STATUTE OF LIMITATIONS

As we discussed in Chapter Four, if you are having problems with your employer, you cannot just go out and file a lawsuit. First, you have to make your employer aware of the problem and give him/her the opportunity to correct the situation. If your employer does not take any action, or if the action taken is not helpful, then you need to file a charge with the EEOC. There are very strict time deadlines for filing the charge. If you do not file the charge in time, you may not be able to file a lawsuit at all. If you cannot file a lawsuit, then you may not be able to get your job back, or receive some form of compensation for your problems.

The time period for filing an EEOC may change depending on whether or not you live in a state with its own independent agency. However, since this book is written to apply nationally, and since the independent states may have different rules, the one safe rule to follow is FILE YOUR "CHARGE" OR COMPLAINT WITH THE EEOC WITHIN 180 DAYS OF THE PROBLEM OR INCIDENT. You will never go wrong by following the 180 day rule.

Beware of an employer who says, "Don't go to the EEOC, we can handle this internally." Quite frankly, they are probably lying. They will drag out their "internal" investigation and reassure you that the situation is being handled. Then, 181 days later, you will find that your situation has not been resolved and you have lost your opportunity and ability to complain.

Knowing to file a charge within 180 days is half the battle. You also need to know when the 180 days starts to run. In other words, what is the incident or problem that starts the time clock?

To be safe, make sure you file the charge within 180 days of the first problem. For instance, I previously discussed my client afflicted with the H.I.V. virus, whose employer refused to give him time off to go to medical appointments and ultimately fired him. This is a violation of the Family Medical Leave Act.

Let's say that my client first requested time off for an appointment on January 1, 1998. His employer denied the request. On February 1, 1998, March 1, 1998 and April 1, 1998, his employer continued to refuse to allow him to take time off for his medical appointments. To be safe, the employee should file his charge with the EEOC 180 days from January 1, 1998. If he doesn't, he may be prevented from introducing evidence on any problems that occurred before the six months. Although there are some rules that allow prior acts to be included, even if they are not timely, you are much better off being safe and filing within 180 days of the first incident.

Let's say the employee filed his initial charge on April 15, 1998. On April 30, 1998, the employer fires him. Now, the employee has 180 days from April 30, 1998 to file another charge for the termination. (The charge may also include a complaint of retaliation against the employee for filing the first charge). Remember, every incident is separate, so if the employee fails to go back to the EEOC and file the termination complaint in a timely manner, he/she may be prevented from bringing that fact into a lawsuit.

Sometimes, employees may not know they were treated unfairly at work until long after the fact. For example, I previously discussed the client whose employer was using the polygraph examination to disqualify African-American applicants. At the time my client applied for the job and was disqualified because of the polygraph, she thought the denial was legitimate. It was not until several years later that she learned that the manager in charge of the hiring was discriminating against African-Americans and using the polygraph examination as an excuse to deny job opportunities. As soon as my client found out, she filed a claim with the EEOC. Now, remember, this is several years after the actual incident, but she had only recently discovered the truth about the employer's actions. She was therefore allowed to file her claim. This was because an employee may not always know at the time that he/she was, in fact, being treated in an unlawful manner.

The employer may hide the real reason for their actions. In such situations, the deadline to file a claim is extended until 180 days after the employee either discovered or reasonably should have discovered that they were discriminated against.

Extending the time deadline in certain cases where the employee does not discover the discrimination until later is a way of protecting innocent employees. However, do not count on the courts being sympathetic if you actually knew or should have known of the problem earlier. In these situations, the courts generally will not extend the 180 day deadline.

Follow the motto "Better safe than sorry." If you believe you are being treated unfairly at work, and you have complained to your employer who has done nothing, file your charge with the EEOC immediately. Your job may depend on it.

A. FILING YOUR EEOC CHARGE

The most important thing to remember when preparing your "charge" or complaint, is that your federal lawsuit can only address issues and individuals that were first raised by the EEOC complaint. For this reason, it is important to continue to file charges against your employer if you continue to have problems. Based on the EEOC's filing requirements, it would be wise to consult an attorney before filing your charge. The attorney can write the charge to make sure that you do not forget about certain individuals or claims, and guarantee that your charge is thorough and complete. The charge must contain the following:

(1) it must be in writing;
(2) it must state the important facts;
(3) specify all dates;
(4) indicate what unlawful employment practice you are complaining of (i.e. age discrimination, sexual harassment); and
(5) it must precisely identify the individuals involved.

B. THE RIGHT TO SUE LETTER

After you correctly file your charge with the EEOC, you will receive a "Right To Sue" letter. This allows you to file a Federal lawsuit. There is also another crucial deadline you must remember:

You must file your federal lawsuit within 90 days of receiving your right to sue letter. If you do not file your lawsuit within the ninety day period, you may lose your right to sue.

CASE EXAMPLE:

A man came to me with a serious problem. He had a strong case of age discrimination and had filed his complaint with the EEOC. He received his right to sue letter on June 30. He filed his lawsuit on September 30, without consulting an attorney. He thought that ninety days meant three months. Therefore, his lawsuit was actually filed two days too late, since there are thirty-one days in July and August. My client came to me after his employer filed a motion to dismiss the lawsuit based on an untimely filing. I fought the case as well as I could- arguing that the case should be decided on the facts, not whether my client missed the deadline by two insignificant days. Unfortunately, the Court did not agree with me.

In the court system, ninety days means ninety days. This is true with all deadlines. You cannot afford to miss a deadline. It could ruin any hope for recovery or victory against your employer.

6. THE LITIGATION PROCESS AND HOW TO CHOOSE THE RIGHT ATTORNEY

A. THE ATTORNEY

If all your efforts to resolve your problems at work have been unsuccessful, you may decide that you need to file a lawsuit. If so, you need to hire an attorney to properly represent your interests.

Unfortunately, the legal profession has taken a big blow to its reputation. I believe this is due, in part, to the fact that there are too many lawyers who do not know what they are doing. Attorneys are taking cases in which they do not have any expertise just so they can stay in business.

Law, like medicine, is a very specialized field. Throughout my many years practicing law, 90% of my cases have involved employment and discrimination issues. Therefore, I have developed a strong background in the area and am well aware of the procedural problems an unqualified attorney would fall into. On the other hand, if I attempted to represent a client in a bankruptcy case, I would be severely disadvantaged—especially if I was up against an opponent who had extensive experience in bankruptcy.

Typically, employment litigation is an area where the employers hire law firms that specialize in employment litigation. Therefore, an employee that fails to go with an equally specialized attorney may be at a great disadvantage.

When deciding on an attorney, your best bet is to retain someone who has been referred to you as having experience in the area. You may contact your local Equal Employment Opportunities Commission to attempt to get a referral. Other special interest groups such as the National Organization for Women (N.O.W.) or the National Association for the Advancement of Colored People (N.A.A.C.P.) may also be able to refer you to a qualified attorney. If you are represented by a union, you should ask your union representative for a referral.

Typically, if you want to hire an attorney, the attorney will request a retainer up front. A retainer is a one time, up-front payment of a certain amount. The amount may differ significantly between attorneys. Some may only request five hundred dollars

($500) and some may require ten thousand ($10,000). Before making an appointment with an attorney, you should ask what their retainer fee is and decide if you can afford it. It is rare for an attorney to waive their retainer fee.

You will usually hire the attorney on a "contingency" basis. This means that, in addition to the retainer, you agree to give the attorney a percentage of anything you receive from the case by way of trial or settlement. This percentage amount varies between attorneys. It may be as low as thirty percent (30%) or as high as forty five percent (45%).

The alternative to a contingency agreement is an agreement to pay the attorney's hourly billing. This is an extremely unusual method for a civil rights plaintiff and would be extremely expensive. An attorney usually charges anywhere from one hundred and fifty dollars ($150) to three hundred and fifty dollars ($350) an hour, and spends hundreds upon hundreds of hours of time on a standard civil rights case.

Typically, you will have an opportunity to meet with the attorney and discuss your case with him/her. This will give you the chance to get a feel for the attorney and determine whether or not you believe you can work with them. Remember, though, that you are hiring the attorney for their legal opinion. An attorney that gets wrapped up in your case emotionally and does not focus on the legal reality would not be in your best interest. You need someone who can stay focused on the issues and get you the results that are both realistic and what you want.

Do not hesitate to ask the attorney questions about your case and get his/her opinion about its strengths and weaknesses. A good attorney will tell you "the good, the bad and the ugly." Do not be surprised if the things that you thought were the most important part of your case are not significant to the attorney. The attorney is looking at your case from a legal perspective. He/she will be able to tell you what is important and what is not.

Important questions to ask the attorney are how he/she plans to litigate the case and whether he/she intends to take depositions. A deposition is where a person is placed under oath and asked questions concerning the case. It takes place before you go to trial and is critical to your case. I cannot emphasize this enough.

If an attorney does not take depositions of the other side, it is the same as going to trial blind. I guarantee that your employer will take your deposition. They will know everything about your life and every tiny aspect of your case. They will then try to use the deposition at trial to trivialize and discredit you.

If your prospective attorney says that depositions are not necessary in employment cases, I suggest you walk out. Even though they are expensive and time consuming, I believe they are absolutely necessary to have any chance of success at trial.

Another question to ask the prospective attorney is how the judge and jury effects a trial. An up-front attorney will admit that a "bad" judge or jury can destroy your trial. The unfortunate fact is that many people do not, or cannot, admit that discrimination, sexual harassment, and unlawful employment practices exist. They are extremely sympathetic to the employer. In fact, the Court of Appeals has forbidden a Federal Court Judge, currently sitting on the bench, from handling police misconduct cases because of the judge's obvious bias in favor of the Police Department. If you get this type of judge, you are in trouble.

The bottom line is do not rush into a decision to hire an attorney. I tell all my clients to talk to other attorneys before they retain me. That way, they can compare what I have to say with other attorneys. If they feel comfortable with the things I tell them, then they can retain me.

Beware, though, of the attorney who tries to tell you everything you want to hear. Remember, I said that an attorney will tell you "the good, the bad, and the ugly." Trust me, every case has some bad and ugly. Every case comes to me mixed with information that is not relevant and potentially destructive to the case. If an attorney is giving you a one hundred percent glowing picture of your lawsuit, he/she may simply be trying to push you into retaining him/her, or may not know what he/she is talking about.

Finally, make sure that you and the attorney understand what you want from your case. I always ask prospective clients what they want. They always say "I want justice" or "I just want an apology." I then say "that's fine, but what do you really want?" Because I know that in a year, when I bring them an offer to settle the case for a reasonable amount of money, all of a sudden the client will think he/she deserves a million dollars. Clients think a lawsuit means they hit the jackpot. This is not the case. Make sure you honestly express to the attorney what you want out of the case, and make sure he/she agrees that your objectives are reasonable.

Ultimately, you will have to decide if you trust the attorney and want to proceed with a lawsuit. Remember, however, that a lawsuit is not easy. I tell my clients that a lawsuit is like a divorce. There is a very slim possibility that you will emerge with a relationship with your employer intact. You need to be willing to "declare war" on you employer and then hold on for some potentially rocky weather.

But a word of caution: DO NOT QUIT YOUR JOB IF YOU ARE GOING TO FILE A LAWSUIT. Your continued position and presence within the company is your strongest bargaining chip for an early and quick resolution of the case. Your employer knows that even if they fight you, and even if they lose, you will still have your job with the company. Any effort to fire you would be retaliation which would put them right back in court. I always advise my clients to hang on to their job unless it seriously threatens their physical or emotional health.

B. THE LAWSUIT

Once you have retained an attorney, the actual legal process is slow and detailed. If your case involves unfair employment practices such as discrimination, violation of the American's with Disability Act, or violation of the Family Medical Leave Act, your attorney will file a claim with either the Equal Employment Opportunity Commission (EEOC) or an equivalent state agency, if appropriate. Both groups oversee employment issues, however, the EEOC is for federal claims and the state agency is for state claims. Your attorney will decide which agency to file with and will frequently file with both.

Once you have filed your claim, the agency may either investigate your case or issue you a "Right to Sue" letter. In employment cases, a Right to Sue letter from either the EEOC or State agency is necessary before continuing with your actual lawsuit. Since the pre-litigation issues concerning EEOC and state claims are critical to a case, they have been discussed in detail in Chapter Four. However, for the purposes of this chapter, you only need to remember that before you can proceed with your lawsuit, you must first file a claim and receive a "Right to Sue Letter."

Once the lawsuit is filed, the defendant (your employer) has a period of time to respond. They must then either file an answer to the lawsuit or file a motion to dismiss.

A motion to dismiss challenges the legitimacy of the lawsuit based "on its face." This means that the Court will determine whether, if everything in the lawsuit can be proven, you have a legitimate case. The motion involves a hearing in front of the court where the attorneys can argue their positions. The court will then either let the lawsuit proceed and order the defendant to answer, or it will grant defendant's motion and possibly permit the plaintiff to have an opportunity to re-draft the complaint.

After you have climbed over the first hurdle of a lawsuit and survived the initial attack by the defendant, you move into the "discovery" phase. The basic purpose of discovery is to remove any element of surprise from the case. Discovery allows both sides to get a clear picture of the other side's case, thereby making it easier to settle before trial. Discovery, if done properly, virtually eliminates the possibility of the classic courtroom scene where an attorney at trial boldly walks up to the witness stand and says, "You, sir, are a racist!!!" and holds up a written document filled with racist and derogatory statements, to the gasps and amazement of everyone watching.

Discovery removes the unknown elements and

also solidifies each side's case. At trial, you can not contradict a response given in discovery. If you do, the jury is instructed to look at the contradiction with suspicion. Therefore, it is critical that you take the discovery process seriously and cooperate with your attorney to provide the best responses possible.

During discovery, your employer can request that you respond to a series of questions, called "interrogatories." You may also be required to provide documents in your possession or control, or give testimony under oath at a deposition.

Frequently, I have clients who get upset by the discovery process. They get irritated by having to take sometimes significant amounts of time to give thoughtful and detailed responses to interrogatories. They get offended by the personal questions which the defendant's attorney may ask.

For example, one married client of mine found out that the defendant was taking the deposition of his girlfriend. Since the girlfriend was a co-worker and had relevant testimony, there was nothing that could be done to prevent it. Did the defendant take the deposition to aggravate my client rather than seek valuable information? Probably. Can they do that? Generally, yes.

The litigation process is not a friendly undertaking. There are some unscrupulous attorneys, and there are other attorneys who are just doing the best job they can to protect their client. Unfortunately, you must accept the good and the bad of litigation.

You may be compensated for your employer's wrongdoing, but you must be willing to accept the road that will take you there.

After discovery is completed, and generally about one month before trial, a defendant in an employment discrimination case will usually file a Motion for Summary Judgment or some form of motion to terminate the your case. This is a critical moment in the case. Unfortunately, employment discrimination cases have one of the highest chances of being thrown out of court. (Four words: Paula Jones-Bill Clinton). This motion is similar to the Motion to Dismiss discussed earlier, however, it is based on the evidence obtained through the discovery process rather than simply what was alleged in the lawsuit. The employee must prove that he/she has evidence to support his/her claims, and demonstrate that there are enough facts to prove the case.

Many times, the decision in the Summary Judgment will cause a case to settle. Since employers know there is a high possibility that the case will be dismissed by the court, they are typically reluctant to offer any kind of significant amount for settlement before a hearing on the motion. However, if the case does survive, the employer is usually well-aware that, given a sympathetic jury, a verdict for the employee can be substantial. Therefore, they want to minimize their chances of exposure and settle the case.

If your employer offers to settle the case, your

attorney should advise you and recommend whether or not you should accept the settlement. Think very carefully before turning down any reasonable settlement offer, however. I tell all my clients to ask themselves two questions if a settlement offer is received:

(1) Can they guarantee that they will win more at trial? (no one can), and
(2) If they cannot guarantee that they will win more, would they rather walk away with nothing instead of accepting the current offer?

This may seem like a ridiculous set of questions, but it is not. I had one client receive a settlement offer for two hundred thousand dollars ($200,000). She had never had so much money in her life at one time. Unfortunately, she got caught up in the idea of belonging to the "million dollar" club, and turned down the offer, despite my repeated warnings. The result? She lost at trial. She got nothing. Do not let this happen to you.

It generally takes anywhere from one to two years to get to trial. If the case actually goes to trial, a jury will decide your case. Even if you win at trial, your employer can still file an appeal. This adds another one to two years before you receive anything.

As you can see, the litigation process is slow and demanding. I do not say this to discourage an employee who has been treated unfairly by his/her employer from filing a lawsuit. It is simply important to have all the information in front of you before making the serious commitment to a lawsuit. Only you can decide what the right decision is.

RUTH

7 SUMMING IT UP

There is a lot of information you need to know in order to protect your rights in the workplace. What I have provided in this book is the fundamentals to start you off.

In the future, I intend to draw on my years of experience as an attorney and share the information that I have learned with you. This will be through seminars, CD-rom discs, and other services.

I hope this book helped you gain the strength and knowledge necessary to ensure that your workplace is a fair and positive place to work. Too much time is spent at work to have to suffer under unfair conditions. I look forward to providing you with additional tools in the future to help you achieve the happiness and job satisfaction you deserve.

For more information, I may be contacted at any of the following:

My website address is: www.LeoTerrell.com

My E-mail address is: leo@leoterrell.com

or send your correspondence to:
    P.O. Box 16254,
    Beverly Hills, California 90209.

A CONTACTING THE EEOC

E-mail address: http://www.eeoc.gov

HEADQUARTERS

U.S. Equal Employment Opportunity Commission
1801 L Street, NW.
Washington, D.C. 20507
Phone: 202-663-4900
TDD: 202-663-4494

FIELD OFFICES

To be automatically connected with the nearest EEOC field office,
Phone: 1-800-669-4000
TDD: 1-800-669-6820

Albuquerque District Office:
505 Marquette Street, N.W.
Suite 900
Albuquerque, NM 87102
Phone: 505-248-5201
TDD: 505-248-5240

Atlanta District Office:
100 Alabama Street
Suite 4R30
Atlanta, GA 30303
Phone: 404-562-6800
TDD: 404-562-6801

Baltimore District Office:
City Crescent Building
10 South Howard Street
3rd Floor
Baltimore, MD 21201
Phone: 410-962-3932
TDD: 410-962-6065

Birmingham District Office:
1900 3rd Avenue, North
Suite 101
Birmingham, AL 35203-2397
Phone: 205-731-1359
TDD: 205-731-0095

Boston Area Office:
1 Congress Street
10th Floor, Room 1001
Boston, MA 02114
Phone: 617-565-3200
TDD: 617-565-3204

Buffalo Local Office:
6 Fountain Plaza
Suite 350
Buffalo, NY 14202
Phone: 716-846-4441
TDD: 716-846-5923

Charlotte District Office:
129 West Trade Street
Suite 400
Charlotte, NC 28202
Phone: 704-344-6682
TDD: 704-344-6684

Chicago District Office:
500 West Madison Street
Suite 2800
Chicago, IL 60661
Phone: 312-353-2713
TDD: 312-353-2421

Cincinnati Area Office:
525 Vine Street
Suite 810
Cincinnati, 011 45202-3122
Phone: 513-684-2851
TDD: 513-684-2074

Cleveland District Office:
1660 West Second Street
Suite 850
Cleveland, OH 44113-1454
Phone: 216-522-2001
TDD: 216-522-8441

Dallas District Office:
207 5. Houston Street
3rd Floor
Dallas, TX 75202-4726
Phone: 214-655-3355
TDD: 214-655-3363

Denver District Office:
303 E. 17th Avenue
Suite 510
Denver, CO 80203
Phone: 303-866-1300
TDD: 303-866-1950

Detroit District Office:
477 Michigan Avenue
Room 865
Detroit, MI 48226-9704
Phone: 313-226-7636
TDD: 313-226-7599

El Paso Area Office:
The Commons, Building C, Suite 100
4171 N. Mesa Street
El Paso, TX 79902
Phone: 915-534-6550
TDD: 915-534-6545

Fresno Local Office:
1265 West Shaw Avenue
Suite 103
Fresno, CA 93711
Phone: 209-487-5793
TDD: 209-487-5837

Greensboro Local Office:
801 Summit Avenue
Greensboro, NC 27405-7813
Phone: 910-333-5174
TDD: 910-333-5542

Greenville Local Office:
Wachovia Building, Suite 530
15 South Main Street
Greenville, SC 29601
Phone: 803-241-4400
TDD: 803-241-4403

Honolulu Local Office:
300 Ala Moana Boulevard, Room 7123-A
P.O. Box 50082
Honolulu, HI 96850-0051
Phone: 808-541-3120
TDD: 808-541-3131

Houston District Office:
1919 Smith Street
7th Floor
Houston, TX 77002
Phone: 713-209-3320
TDD: 713-209-3367

Indianapolis District Office:
101 W. Ohio Street
Suite 1900
Indiana, IN 46204-4203
Phone: 317-226-7212
TDD: 317-226-5162

Jackson Area Office:
207 West Amite Street
Jackson, MS 39201
Phone: 601-965-4537
TDD: 601-965-4915

Kansas City Area Office:
400 State Avenue
Suite 905
Kansas City, KS 66101
Phone: 913-551-5655
TDD: 913-551-5657

Little Rock Area Office:
425 West Capitol Avenue
Suite 625
Little Rock, AR 72201
Phone: 501-324-5060
TDD: 501-324-5481

Los Angeles District Office:
255 E. Temple
4th Floor
Los Angeles, CA 90012
Phone: 213-894-1000
TDD: 213-894-1121

Louisville Area Office:
600 Dr. Martin Luther King Jr. Place
Suite 268
Louisville, KY 40202
Phone: 502-582-6082
TDD: 502-582-6285

Memphis District Office:
1407 Union Avenue
Suite 521
Memphis, TN 38104
Phone: 901-544-0115
TDD: 901-544-0112

Miami District Office:
One Biscayne Tower
2 South Biscayne Boulevard
Suite 2700
Miami, FL 33131
Phone: 305-536-4491
TDD: 305-536-5721

Milwaukee District Office:
310 West Wisconsin Avenue
Suite 800
Milwaukee, WI 53203-2292
Phone: 414-297-1111
TDD: 414-297-1115

Minneapolis Area Office:
330 South Second Avenue
Suite 430
Minneapolis, MN 55401-2224
Phone: 612-335-4040
TDD: 612-335-4045

Nashville Area Office:
50 Vantage Way
Suite 202
Nashville, TN 37228
Phone: 615-736-5820
TDD: 615-736-5870

Newark Area Office:
1 Newark Center
21st Floor
Newark, NJ 07102-5233
Phone: 201-645-6383
TDD: 201-645-3004

New Orleans District Office:
701 Loyola Avenue
Suite 600
New Orleans, LA 70113-9936
Phone: 504-589-2329
TDD: 504-589-2958

New York District Office:
7 World Trade Center
18th Floor
New York, NY 10048-0948
Phone: 212-748-8500
TDD: 212-748-8399

Norfolk Area Office:
World Trade Center
101 West Main Street
Suite 4300
Norfolk, VA 23510
Phone: 804-441-3470
TDD: 804-441-3578

Oakland Local Office:
1301 Clay Street
Suite 1170-N
Oakland, CA 94612-5217
Phone: 510-637-3230
TDD: 510-637-3234

Oklahoma Area Office:
210 Park Avenue
Oklahoma City, OK 73102
Phone: 405-231-4911
TDD: 405-231-5745

Philadelphia District Office:
21 South 5th Street
4th Floor
Philadelphia, PA 19106
Phone: 215-451-5800
TDD: 215-451-5814

Phoenix District Office:
3300 N. Central Avenue
Phoenix, AZ 85012-] 848
Phone: 602-640-5000
TDD: 602-640-5072

Pittsburgh Area Office:
1001 Liberty Avenue
Suite 300
Pittsburgh, PA 15222-4187
Phone: 412-644-3444
TDD: 412-644-2720

Raleigh Area Office:
1309 Annapolis Drive
Raleigh, NC 27608-2129
Phone: 919-856-4064
TDD: 919-856-4296

Richmond Area Office:
3600 West Broad Street
Room 229
Richmond, VA 23230
Phone: 804-278-4651
TDD: 804-278-4654

San Antonio District Office:
5410 Fredericksburg Road
Suite 200
San Antonio, TX 78229-3555
Phone: 210-229-4810
TDD: 210-229-4858

San Diego Area Office:
401 B Street
Suite 1550
San Diego, CA 92101
Phone: 619-557-7235
TDD: 619-557-7232

San Francisco District Office:
901 Market Street
Suite 500
San Francisco, CA 94103
Phone: 415-356-5100
TDD: 415-356-5098

San Jose Local Office
96 North 3rd Street
Suite 200
San Jose, CA 95112
Phone: 408-291-7352
TDD: 408-291-7374

Savannah Local Office:
410 Mall Boulevard
Suite G
Savannah, GA 31406-4821
Phone: 912-652-4234
TDD: 912-652-4439

Seattle District Office:
Federal Office Building, Suite 400
909 First Avenue
Seattle, WA 98104-1061
Phone: 206-220-6883
TDD: 206-220-6882

St. Louis District Office:
Robert A. Young Building
122 Spruce Street
Room 8.100
St. Louis, MO 63103
Phone: 314-539-7800
TDD: 314-539-7803

Tampa Area Office:
501 East Polk Street
10th Floor
Tampa, FL 33602
Phone: 813-228-2310
TDD: 813-228-2003

Washington Field Office:
1400 L Street, N.W.
Suite 200
Phone: 202-275-7377
TDD: 202-275-7518

B 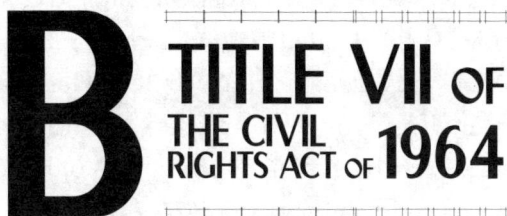 TITLE VII OF THE CIVIL RIGHTS ACT OF 1964

42 U.S.C.A. §§2000e-2000e-17

§2000e. [§701] Definitions
For the purposes of this subchapter-

(a) The term "person" includes one or more individuals, governments, governmental agencies, political subdivisions, labor unions, partnerships, associations, corporations, legal representatives, mutual companies, joint-stock companies, trusts, unincorporated organizations, trustees, trustees in cases under title 11, United States Code, or receivers.

(b) The term "employer" means a person engaged in an industry affecting commerce who has fifteen or more employees for each working day in each of twenty or more calendar weeks in the current or preceding calendar year, and any agent of such a person, but such term does not include (1) the United States, a corporation wholly owned by the Government of the United States, an Indian tribe, or any department or agency of the District of Columbia subject by statute to procedures of the competitive service (as defined in section 2102 of Title 5), or (2) a bona fide private membership club (other than a labor organization) which is exempt from taxation under section 501(c) of Title 26 [the Internal Revenue Code of 1954], except that during the first year after March 24, 1972, persons having fewer than twenty-five employees (and their agents) shall not be considered employers.

(c) The term "employment agency" means any person regularly undertaking with or without compensation to procure employees for an employer or to procure for employees opportunities to work for employer and includes an agent of such a person.

(d) The term "labor organization" means a labor organization engaged in an industry affecting commerce, and any agent of such an organization, and includes any organization of any kind, any agency, or employee representation committee, group, association, or plan so engaged in which employees participate and which exists for the purpose, in whole or in part, of dealing with employers concerning grievances, labor disputes, wages, rates of pay, hours, or other terms of conditions of employment, and any conference, general committee, joint or system board, or joint council so engaged which is subordinate to a national or international labor organization.

(e) A labor organization shall be deemed to be engaged in an industry affecting commerce if (1) it maintains or operates a hiring hall or hiring office which procures employees for an employer or procures for employees opportunities to work for an employer, or (2) the number of its members (or, where it is a labor organization composed of other labor organizations or their representatives, if the aggregate number of the members of such other labor organization) is

(A) twenty-five or more during the first year after March 24, 1972, or

(B) fifteen or more thereafter, and such labor organization-

(1) is the certified representative of employees under the provisions of the National Labor Relations Act [29 U.S.C. §§151-168], as amended, or the Railway Labor Act [45 U.S.C. §§151-188], as amended;

(2) although not certified, is a national or international labor organization or a local labor organization recognized or acting as the representative of employees of an employer or employers engaged in an industry affecting commerce; or

(3) has chartered a local labor organization or subsidiary body which is representing or actively seeking to represent employees of employers within the meaning of paragraph (1) or (2); or

(4) has been chartered by a labor organization representing or actively seeking to represent employees within the meaning of paragraph (1) or (2) as the local or subor-

dinate body through which such employees may enjoy membership or become affiliated with such labor organization; or

(5) is a conference, general committee, joint or system board, or joint council subordinate to a national or international labor organization, which includes a labor organization engaged in an industry affecting commerce within the meaning of any of the preceding paragraphs of this subsection.

(f) The term "employee" means an individual employed by an employer, except that the term "employee" shall not include any person elected to public office in any State or political subdivision of any State by the qualified voters thereof, or any person chosen by such officer to be on such officer's personal staff, or an appointee on the policy making level or an immediate adviser with respect to the exercise of the constitutional or legal powers of the office. The exemption set forth in the preceding sentence shall not include employees subject to the civil service laws of a State government, governmental agency or political subdivision. With respect to employment in a foreign country, such term includes an individual who is a citizen of the United States.

[Sec. 2000e(f) amended by Civil Rights Act of 1991, Pub. L. No. 102- 166, §l09, 105 Stat. 1077]

(g) The term "commerce" means trade, traffic, commerce, transportation, transmission, or communication among the several States; or between a State and any place outside thereof; or within the District of Columbia, or a possession of the United States; or between points in the same State but through a point outside thereof.

(h) The term "industry affecting commerce: means any activity, business, or industry affecting commerce or in which a labor dispute would hinder or obstruct commerce or the free flow of commerce and includes any activity or industry "affecting commerce" within the meaning of the Labor-Management Reporting and Disclosure Act of 1959, and further includes any governmental industry, business, or activity.

(i) The term "State" includes a State of the United States, the District of Columbia, Puerto Rico, the Virgin Islands, American
Samoa, Guam, Wake Island, the Canal Zone, and Outer Continental Shelf lands defined in the Outer Continental Shelf Lands Act.

(j) The term "religion" includes all aspects of religious observance and practice, as well as belief, unless an employer demonstrates that he is unable to reasonably accommodate to an employee's or prospective employee's religious observance or practice without undue hardship on the conduct of the employer's business.

(k) The terms "because of sex" or "on the basis of sex" include, but are not limited to, because of or on the basis of pregnancy, childbirth, or related medical conditions; and women affected by pregnancy, childbirth, or related medical conditions shall be treated the same for all employment-related purposes, including receipt of benefits under fringe benefit programs, as other persons not so affected but similar in their ability or inability to work, and nothing in section 2000e-2(h) of this title shall be interpreted to permit otherwise. This subsection shall not require an employer to pay for health insurance benefits for abortion, except where the life of the mother would be endangered if the fetus were carried to term, or except where medical complications have arisen from an abortion: Provided, that nothing herein shall preclude an employer from providing abortion benefits or otherwise affect bargaining agreements in regard to abortion.

(l) The term "complaining party" means the Commission, the Attorney General, or a person who may bring an action or proceeding under this title.

(m) The term "demonstrates" means meets the burdens of production and persuasion.

(n) The term "respondent" means an employer, employment agency, labor organization, joint labor-management committee controlling apprenticeship or other training or retraining program, including an on-the-job training program, or Federal entity subject to section 717. [Sec. 2000e(l)-(m) amended by Civil Rights Act of 1991, Pub. L. No. 102-166, §104, 105 Stat. 1074]

§2000e-1. [§702] (a) Subchapter not applicable to employment of aliens outside State and individuals for performance of activities of religious corporations, associations, educational institutions, or societies

This subchapter shall not apply to an employer with respect to the employment of aliens outside any State, or to a religious corporation, association, educational institution, or society with respect to the employment of individuals of a particular religion to perform work connected with the carrying on by such corporation, association, educational institution, or society of its activities.

(b) It shall not be unlawful under section 703 or 704 for an employer (or a corporation controlled by an employer), labor organization, employment agency, or joint labor-management committee controlling apprenticeship or other training or retraining (including on-the-job training programs) to take any action otherwise prohibited by such section, with respect to an employee in a workplace in a foreign country if compliance with such section would cause such employer (or such corporation), such organization, such agency, or such committee to violate the law of the foreign country in which such workplace is located.

(c)(1) If an employer controls a corporation whose place of incorporation is a foreign country, any practice prohibited by section 703 or 704 engaged in by such corporation shall be presumed to be engaged in by such employer.

(2) Sections 703 and 704 shall not apply with respect to the foreign operations of an employer that is a foreign person not controlled by an American employer.

(3) For purposes of this subsection, the determination of whether an employer controls a corporation shall be based on

(A) the interrelation of operations;

(B) the common management;

(C) the centralized control of labor relations; and

(D) the common ownership or financial control, of the

employer and the corporation.
[Sec. 2000e-1(b)-(c) amended by Civil Rights Act of 1991, Pub. L. No. 102-166, §109, 105 Stat. 1077]

§2000e-2. [§703] Unlawful employment practices

Employer practices

(a) It shall be an unlawful employment practice for an employer-

(1) to fail or refuse to hire or to discharge any individual, or otherwise to discriminate against any individual with respect to his compensation, terms, conditions, or privileges of employment, because of such individual's race, color, religion, sex, or national origin; or

(2) to limit, segregate, or classify his employees or applicants for employment in any way which would deprive or tend to deprive any individual of employment opportunities or otherwise adversely affect his status as an employee, because of such individual's race, color, religion, sex, or national origin.

Employment agency practices

(b) It shall be an unlawful employment practice for an employment agency to fail or refuse to refer for employment, or otherwise to discriminate against, any individual because of his race, color, religion, sex, or national origin, or to classify or refer for employment, or otherwise to discriminate against, any individual because of his race, color, religion, sex, or national origin, or to classify or refer for employment any individual on the basis of his race, color, religion, sex, or national origin.

Labor organization practices

(c) It shall be an unlawful employment practice for a labor organization-

(1) to exclude or to expel from its membership, or otherwise to discriminate against, any individual because of his race, color, religion, sex, or national origin;

(2) to limit, segregate, or classify its membership or applicants for membership, or to classify or fail or refuse to refer for employment any individual, in any way which would deprive or tend to deprive any individual of employment opportunities, or would limit such employment opportunities or otherwise adversely affect his status as an employee or as an applicant for employment, because of such individual's race, color, religion, sex, or national origin; or

(3) to cause or attempt to cause an employer to discriminate against an individual in violation of this section.

Training programs

(d) It shall be an unlawful employment practice for any employer, labor organization, or joint labor-management committee controlling apprenticeship or other training or retraining, including on-the-job training programs to discriminate against any individual because of his race, color, religion, sex, or national origin in admission to, or employment in, any program established to provide apprenticeship or other training.

Businesses or enterprises with personnel qualified on basis of religion, sex, or national origin; educational institutions with personnel of particular religion

(e) Notwithstanding any other provision of this subchapter, (1) It shall not be an unlawful employment practice for an employer to hire and employ employees, for an employment agency to classify, or refer for employment any individual, for a labor organization to classify its membership or to classify or refer for employment any individual, or for an employer, labor organization, or joint labor-management committee controlling apprenticeship or other training or retraining programs to admit or employ any individual in any such program, on the basis of his religion, sex, or national origin in those certain instances where religion, sex, or national origin is a bona fide occupational qualification reasonably necessary to the normal operation of that particular business or enter-

practice for a school, college, university, or other educational institution or institution of learning to hire and employ employees of a particular religion if such school, college, university, or other educational institution or institution of learning is, in whole or in substantial part, owned, supported, controlled, or managed by a particular religion or by a particular religious corporation, association, or society, or if the curriculum of such school, college, university, or other educational institution or institution of learning is directed toward the propagation of a particular religion.

Members of Communist Party or Communist-action or Communist-front organizations

(f) As used in this subchapter, the phrase "unlawful employment practice" shall not be deemed to include any action or measure taken by an employer, labor organization, joint labor-management committee, or employment agency with respect to an individual who is a member of the Communist Party of the United States or of any other organization required to register as a Communist-action or Communist-front organization by final order of the Subversive Activities Control Board pursuant to the Subversive Activities Control Act of 1950.

National security

(g) Notwithstanding any other provision of this subchapter, it shall not be an unlawful employment practice for an employer to fail or refuse to hire and employ any individual for any position, for an employer to discharge any individual from any position, or for an employment agency to fail or refuse to refer any individual for employment in any position, or for a labor organization to fail or refuse to refer any individual for employment in any position, if-

(1) the occupancy of such position, or access to the premises in or upon which any part of the duties of such position is performed or is to be performed, is subject to any requirement imposed in the interest of the national security of the United States under any security program in effect pursuant to or administered under any statute of the United States or any Executive order of the President;

and

(2) such individual has not fulfilled or has ceased to fulfill that requirement.

Seniority or merit system; quantity or quality of production; ability tests; compensation based on sex and authorized by minimum wage provisions

(h) Notwithstanding any other provision of this subchapter, it shall not be an unlawful employment practice for an employer to apply different standards of compensation, or different terms, conditions, or privileges of employment pursuant to a bona fide seniority or merit system, or a system which measures earnings by quantity or quality of production or to employees who work in different locations, provided that such differences are not the result of an intention to discriminate because of race, color, religion, sex, or national origin, nor shall it be an unlawful employment practice for an employer to give and to act upon the results of any professionally developed ability test provided that such test, its administration or action upon the results is not designed, intended or used to discriminate because of race, color, religion, sex or national origin. It shall not be an unlawful employment practice under this subchapter for any employer to differentiate upon the basis of sex in determining the amount of the wages or compensation paid or to be paid to employees of such employer if such differentiation is authorized by the provisions of section 206(d) of Title 29.

Businesses or enterprises extending preferential treatment to Indians

(i) Nothing contained in this subchapter shall apply to any business or enterprise on or near an Indian reservation with respect to any publicly announced employment practice of such business or enterprise under which a preferential treatment is given to any individual because he is an Indian living on or near a reservation.

Preferential treatment not to be granted on account of existing number or percentage imbalance

(j) Nothing contained in this subchapter shall be interpreted to require any employer, employment agency, labor organization, or joint labor-management committee subject to this subchapter to grant preferential treatment to any individual or to any group because of the race, color, religion, sex, or national origin of such individual or group on account of an imbalance which may exist with respect to the total number or percentage of persons of any race, color, religion, sex, or national origin employed by any employer, referred or classified for employment by any employment agency or labor organization, admitted to membership or classified by any labor organization, or admitted to, or employed in, any apprenticeship or other training program, in comparison with the total number or percentage of persons of such race, color, religion, sex, or national origin in any community, State, section, or other area, or in the available work force in any community, State, section, or other area.

(k)(1)(A) An unlawful employment practice based on

disparate impact is established under this title only if—

(i) a complaining party demonstrates that a respondent uses a particular employment practice that causes a disparate impact on the basis of race, color, religion, sex, or national origin and the respondent fails to demonstrate that the challenged practice is job related for the position in question and consistent with business necessity; or

(ii) the complaining party makes the demonstration described in subparagraph (C) with respect to an alternative employment practice and the respondent refuses to adopt such alternative employment practice.

(B)(i) With respect to demonstrating that a particular employment practice causes a disparate impact as described in subparagraph (A)(i), the complaining party shall demonstrate that each particular challenged employment practice causes a disparate impact, except that if the complaining party can demonstrate to the court that the elements of a respondent's decision making process are not capable of separation for analysis, the decisionmaking process may be analyzed as one employment practice.

(iii) If the respondent demonstrates that a specific employment practice does not cause the disparate impact, the respondent shall not be required to demonstrate that such practice is required by business necessity.

(C) The demonstration referred to by subparagraph (A)(ii) shall be in accordance with the law as it existed on June 4, 1989, with respect to the concept of "alternative employment practice."

(2) A demonstration that an employment practice is required by business necessity may not be used as a

defense against a claim of intentional discrimination under this title.

(3) Notwithstanding any other provision of this title, a rule barring the employment of an individual who currently and knowingly uses or possesses a controlled substance, as defined in schedules I and II of section 102(6) of the Controlled Substances Act (21 U.S.C. 802(6)), other than a use or possession of a drug taken under the supervision of a licensed health care professional, or any other use or possession authorized by the Controlled Substances Act or any other provision of Federal law, shall be considered an unlawful employment practice under this title only if such rule is adopted or applied with an intent to discriminate because of race, color, religion, sex, or national origin.

(b) No statements other than the interpretive memorandum appearing at Vol. 137 Congressional Record 5 15276 (daily ed. Oct. 25, 1991) shall be considered legislative history of, or relied upon in any way as legislative history in construing or applying, any provision of this Act that relates to Wards Cove-Business necessity, cumulation, alternative business practice.
[Sec. 2000e-2(k)(1)(A)-(c) and (b) amended by Civil Rights Act of 1991, Pub. L. No. 102-166, §105, 105 Stat. 1074-75]

(l) It shall be an unlawful employment practice for a respondent, in connection with the selection or referral of applicants or candidates for employment or promotion, to adjust the scores of use different cutoff scores for, or otherwise alter the results of, employment related tests on the basis of race, color, religion, sex, or national origin. [Sec.

2000e-2(l) amended by Civil Rights Act of 1991, Pub. L. No. 102-166, §106, 105 Stat. 1075]

(m) Except as otherwise provided in this title, an unlawful employment practice is established when the complaining party demonstrates that race, color, religion, sex, or national origin was a motivating factor for any employment practice, even though other factors also motivated the practice.

[Sec. 2000e-2(m) amended by Civil Rights Act of 1991, Pub. L. No. 102-166, §107, 105 Stat. 1075]

(n)(1)(A) Notwithstanding any other provision of law, and except as provided in paragraph (2), an employment practice that implements and is within the scope of a litigated or consent judgment or order that resolves a claim of employment discrimination under the Constitution or Federal civil rights laws may not be challenged under the circumstances described in subparagraph (B).

(B) A practice described in subparagraph (A) may not be challenged in a claim under the Constitution or Federal civil rights laws-

(i) by a person who, prior to the entry of the judgment or order described in subparagraph (A), had-

(I) actual notice of the proposed judgment or order sufficient to apprise such person that such judgment or order might adversely affect the interests and legal rights of such person and that an opportunity was available to present objections to such judgment or order by a future date certain; and

(II) a reasonable opportunity to present objections to such judgment or order; or

(ii) by a person whose interests were adequately represented by another person who had previously challenged the judgment or order on the same legal grounds and with a similar factual situation, unless there has been an intervening change in law or fact.

(2) Nothing in this subsection shall be construed to-

(A) alter the standards for intervention under rule 24 of the Federal Rules of Civil Procedure or apply to the rights of parties who have successfully intervened pursuant to such rule in the proceeding in which the parties intervened;

(B) apply to the rights of parties to the action in which a litigated or consent judgment or order was entered, or of members of a class represented or sought to be represented in such action, or of members of a group on whose behalf relief was sought in such action by the Federal Government;

(C) prevent challenges to a litigated or consent judgment or order on the ground that such judgment or order was obtained through collusion or fraud, or is transparently invalid or was entered by a court lacking subject matter jurisdiction; or

(D) authorize or permit the denial to any person of the due process of law required by the Constitution.

(3) Any action not precluded under this subsection that challenges an employment consent judgment or order described in paragraph (1) shall be brought in the court, and if possible before the judge, that entered such judgment or order. Nothing in this subsection shall preclude a transfer of such action pursuant to section 1404 of

title 28, United States Code.

[Sec. 2000e-2(n)(l)-(3) amended by Civil Rights Act of 1991, Pub. L. No. 102-166, §108, 105 Stat. 1076-77]

§2000e-3. [§704] Other unlawful employment practices

Discrimination for making charges, testifying, assisting, or participating in enforcement proceedings

(a) It shall be an unlawful employment practice for an employer to discriminate against any of his employees or applicants for employment, for an employment agency, or joint labor-management committee controlling apprenticeship or other training or retraining, including on-the-job training programs, to discriminate against any individual, or for a labor organization to discriminate against any member thereof or applicant for membership, because he has opposed any practice made an unlawful employment practice by this subchapter, or because he has made a charge, testified, assisted, or participated in any manner in an investigation, proceeding, or hearing under this subchapter.

Printing or publication of notices or advertisements indicating prohibited preference, limitation, specification, or discrimination; occupational qualification exception

(b) It shall be an unlawful employment practice for an employer, labor organization, employment agency, or joint labor-management committee controlling apprenticeship or other training or retraining, including on-the-job training programs, to print or publish or cause to be printed or published any notice or advertisement relating to employment by such an employer or membership in or any classification or referral for employment by such a labor organization, or relating to any classification or referral for employment by such an employment agency, or relating to admission to, or employment in, any program established to provide apprenticeship or other training by such a joint labor-management committee, indicating any preference, limitation, specification, or discrimination, based on race, color, religion, sex, or national origin except that such a notice or advertisement may indicate a preference, limitation, specification, or discrimination based on religion, sex, or national origin when religion, sex, or national origin is a bona fide occupational qualification for employment.

§200Oe4. [§705] Equal Employment Opportunity Commission

Creation; composition; political representation; appointment; term; vacancies; Chairman and Vice Chairman; duties of Chairman; appointment of personnel; compensation of personnel

(a) There is hereby created a Commission to be known as the Equal Employment Opportunity Commission, which shall be composed of five members, not more than three of whom shall be members of the same political party. Members of the Commission shall be appointed by the President by and with the advice and Consent of the Senate for a term of five years. Any individual chosen to fill a vacancy shall be appointed only for the unexpired term of the member whom he shall succeed, and all members of the Commission shall continue to serve until their successors are appointed and qualified, except that no such member of the Commission shall continue to serve (I) for more than sixty days when the Congress is in session unless a nomination to fill such vacancy shall have been submitted to the Senate, or (2) after the adjournment sine die of the session of the Senate in which such nomination was submitted. The President shall designate one member to serve as Chairman of the Commission, and one member to serve as Vice Chairman. The Chairman shall be responsible on behalf of the Commission for the administrative operations of the Commission, and, except as provided in subsection (b) of this Section, shall appoint, in accordance with the provisions of Title 5 governing appointments in the competitive service, such officers, agents, attorneys, administrative law judges, and employees as he deems necessary to assist it in the performance of its functions and to fix their compensation in accordance with the provisions of chapter 51 and subchapter III of chapter 53 of Title 5, relating to classification and General Schedule pay rates: Provided, That assignment, removal, and compensation of administrative law judges shall be in accordance with sections 3105, 3344, 5372, and 7521 of Title 5.

General Counsel; appointment; term; duties; representation by attorneys and Attorney General

(b)(1) There shall be a General Counsel of the Commission appointed by the President, by and with the advice and consent of the Senate, for a term of four years. The General Counsel shall have responsibility for the conduct of litigation as provided in sections 2000e-5 and 2000e-6 of this title. The General Counsel shall have such other duties as the Commission may prescribe or as may be provided by law and shall concur with the Chairman of the Commission on the appointment and supervision of regional attorneys. The General Counsel of the Commission on the effective date of this Act shall continue in such position and perform the functions specified in this subsection until a successor is appointed and qualified.

(2) Attorneys appointed under this section may, at the direction of the Commission, appear for and represent the Commission in any case in court, provided that the Attorney General shall conduct all litigation to which the Commission is a party in the Supreme Court pursuant to this subchapter.

Exercise of powers during vacancy; quorum

(c) A vacancy in the Commission shall not impair the right of the remaining members to exercise all the powers of the Commission and three members thereof shall constitute a quorum.

Seal; judicial notice

(d) The Commission shall have an official seal which shall be judicially noticed.

Reports to Congress and President

(e) The Commission shall at the close of each fiscal year report to the Congress and to the President concerning the action it has taken and the moneys it has disbursed. It shall make such further reports on the cause of and means of eliminating discrimination and such recommendations for further legislation as may appear desirable.

Principal and other offices

(f) The principal office of the Commission shall be in or near the District of Columbia, but it may meet or exercise any or all its powers at any other place. The Commission may establish such regional or State offices as it deems necessary to accomplish the purpose of this subchapter.

Powers of Commission

(g) The Commission shall have power-

(1) to cooperate with and, with their consent, utilize regional, State, local, and other agencies, both public and private, and individuals;

(2) to pay to witnesses whose depositions are taken or who are summoned before the Commission or any of its agents the same witness and mileage fees as are paid to witnesses in the courts of the United States;

(3) to furnish to persons subject to this subchapter such technical assistance as they may request to further their compliance with this subchapter or an order issued thereunder;

(4) upon the request of (i) any employer, whose employees or some of them, or (ii) any labor organization, whose members or some of them, refuse or threaten to refuse to cooperate in effectuating the provisions of this subchapter, to assist in such effectuation by conciliation or such other remedial action as is provided by this subchapter;

(5) to make such technical studies as are appropriate to effectuate the purposes and policies of this subchapter and to make the results of such studies available to the public;

(6) to intervene in a civil action brought under section 2000e-5 of this title by an aggrieved party against a respondent other than a government, governmental agency or political subdivision.

Cooperation with other departments and agencies in performance of educational or promotional activities

(h)(1) The Commission shall, in any of its educational or promotional activities, cooperate with other departments and agencies in the performance of such educational and promotional activities.

(2) In exercising its powers under this title, the Commission shall carry out educational and outreach activities (including dissemination of information in lan-

guages other than English) targeted to-

(A) individuals who historically have been victims of employment discrimination and have not been equitably served by the Commission; and

(B) individuals on whose behalf the Commission has authority to enforce any other law prohibiting employment discrimination, concerning rights and obligations under this title or such law, as the case may be.

[Sec. 2000e-4(h)(2) amended by Civil Rights Act of 1991, Pub. L. No. 102-166, §111, 105 Stat. 1078]

Personnel subject to political activity restrictions

(i) All officers, agents, attorneys, and employees of the Commission shall be subject to the provisions of section 7324 of Title 5, notwithstanding any exemption contained in such section.

(j)(1) The Commission shall establish a Technical Assistance Training Institute, through which the Commission shall provide technical assistance and training regarding the laws and regulations enforced by the Commission.

(2) An employer or other entity covered under this title shall not be excused from compliance with the requirements of this title because of any failure to receive technical assistance under this subsection.

(3) There are authorized to be appropriated to carry out this subsection such sums as may be necessary for fiscal year 1992.

(b) Effective Date.-The amendment made by this section shall take effect on the date of the enactment of this

Act.
[Sec. 2000e-4(j) amended by Civil Rights Act of 1991, Pub. L. No. 102-166, §110, 105 Stat. 1078]

§2000e-5. [706] Enforcement provisions

Power of Commission to prevent unlawful employment practices

(a) The Commission is empowered, as hereinafter provided, to prevent any person from engaging in any unlawful employment practice as set forth in section 2000e-2 or 2000e-3 of this title.

Charges by persons aggrieved or member of Commission of unlawful employment practices by employers, etc.; filing; allegations; notice to respondent; contents of notice; investigation by Commission; contents of charges; prohibition on disclosure of charges; determination of reasonable cause; conference, conciliation, and persuasion for elimination of unlawful practices; prohibition on disclosure of informal endeavors to end unlawful practices; use of evidence in subsequent proceedings; penalties for disclosure of information; time for determination of reasonable cause

(b) Whenever a charge is filed by or on behalf of a person claiming to be aggrieved, or by a member of the Commission, alleging that an employer, employment agency, labor organization, or joint labor-management committee controlling apprenticeship or other training or retraining, including on-the-job training programs, has engaged in an unlawful employment practice, the Commission shall serve a notice of the charge (including the date, place and circumstances of the alleged unlawful employment practice) on such employer, employment agency, labor organization, or joint labor-management committee (hereinafter referred to as the "respondent") within ten days, and shall make an investigation thereof. Charges shall be in writing under oath or affirmation and shall contain such information and be in such form as the Commission requires. Charges shall not be made public by the Commission. If the Commission determines after such investigation that there is not reasonable cause to believe that the charge is true, it shall dismiss the charge and promptly notify the person claiming to be aggrieved and the respondent of its action. In determining whether reasonable cause exists, the Commission shall accord substantial weight to final findings and orders made by State or local authorities in proceedings commenced under State or local law pursuant to the requirements of subsections (c) and (d) of this section. If the Commission determines after such investigation that there is reasonable cause to believe that the charge is true, the Commission shall endeavor to eliminate any such alleged unlawful employment practice by informal methods of conference, conciliation, and persuasion. Nothing said or done during and as a part of such informal endeavors may be made public by the Commission, its officers or employees, or used as evidence in a subsequent proceeding without the written consent of the persons concerned. Any person who makes public information in violation of this subsection shall he fined not more than $1,000 or imprisoned for not more than one year, or both. The Commission shall make its determination on reasonable cause as promptly as possible and, so far as practicable, not later than one hundred and twenty days from the filing of the charge or, where applicable under subsection (c) or (d) of this section, from the date upon which the Commission is authorized to take action with respect to the charge.

State or local enforcement proceedings; notification of State or local authority; time for filing charges with Commission; commencement of proceedings

(c) In the case of an alleged unlawful employment practice occurring in a State, or political subdivision of a State, which has a State or local law prohibiting the unlawful employment practice alleged and establishing or authorizing a State or local authority to grant or seek relief from such practice or to institute criminal proceedings with respect thereto upon receiving notice thereof, no charge may be filed under subsection (b) by the person aggrieved before the expiration of sixty days after proceedings have been commenced under the State or local law, unless such proceedings have been earlier terminated, provided that such sixty-day period shall be extended to one hundred and twenty days during the first year after the effective date of such State or local law. If any requirement for the commencement of such proceedings is imposed by a State or local authority other than a requirement of the filing of a written and signed statement of the facts upon which the proceeding is based, the proceeding shall be deemed to have been commenced for the purposes of this subsection at the time such statement is sent by registered mail to the appropriate State or local authority.

State or local enforcement proceedings; notification of State or local authority; time for action on charges by Commission

(d) In the case of any charge filed by a member of the Commission alleging an unlawful employment practice occurring in a State or political subdivision of a State which has a State or local law prohibiting the practice alleged and establishing or authorizing a State or local authority to grant or seek relief from such practice or to institute criminal proceedings with respect thereto upon receiving notice thereof, the Commission shall, before taking any action with respect to such charge, notify the appropriate State or local officials and, upon request, afford them a reasonable time, but not less than sixty days (provided that such sixty-day period shall be extended to one hundred and twenty days during the first year after the effective day of such State or local law), unless a shorter period is requested, to act under such State or local law to remedy the practice alleged.

Time for filing charges; time for service of notice of charge on respondent; filing of charge by Commission with State or local agency

(e)(1) A charge under this section shall be filed within one hundred and eighty days after the alleged unlawful employment practice occurred and notice of the charge (including the date, place and circumstances of the alleged unlawful employment practice) shall be served upon the person against whom such charge is made within ten days thereafter, except that in a case of an unlawful employment practice with respect to which the person aggrieved has initially instituted proceedings with a State or local agency with authority to grant or seek relief from such practice or to institute criminal proceedings with respect thereto upon receiving notice thereof, such charge shall be filed by or on behalf of the person aggrieved within three hundred days after the alleged unlawful employment practice occurred, or within thirty days after receiving notice that the State or local agency has terminated the proceedings under the State or local law, whichever is earlier, and a copy of such charge shall be filed by the Commission with the State or local agency.

(2) For purposes of this section, an unlawful employment practice occurs, with respect to a seniority system that has been adopted for an intentionally discriminatory purpose in violation of this title (whether or not that discriminatory purpose is apparent on the face of the seniority provision), when the seniority is adopted, when an individual becomes subject to the seniority system, or when a person aggrieved is injured by the application of the seniority system provision of the system.
[Sec. 2000e-5(e)(2) amended by Civil Rights Act of 1991, Pub. L. No. 102-166, §112, 105 Stat. 1079]

Civil action by Commission, Attorney General, or person aggrieved; preconditions; procedure; appointment of attorney; payment of fees, costs, or security; intervention; stay of Federal proceedings; action for appropriate temporary or preliminary relief pending final disposition of charge; jurisdiction and venue of United States courts; designation of judge to hear and determine case; assignment of case for hearing; expedition of case; appointment of master

(f)(l) If within thirty days after a charge is filed with the Commission or within thirty days after expiration of any period of reference under subsection (c) or (d) of this section, the Commission has been unable to secure from the respondent a conciliation agreement acceptable to the Commission, the Commission may bring a civil action against any respondent not a government, governmental agency, or political subdivision named in the charge. In the case of a respondent which is a government, governmental agency, or political subdivision, if the Commission has been unable to secure from the respondent a conciliation agreement acceptable to the Commission, the Commission shall take no further action and shall refer the case to the Attorney General who may bring a civil action against such respondent in the appropriate United States district court. The person or persons aggrieved shall have the right to intervene in a civil action brought by the Commission or the Attorney General in a case involving a government, governmental agency, or political subdivision. If a charge filed with the Commission pursuant to subsection (b) of this section is dismissed by the Commission, or if within one hundred and eighty days from the filing of such charge or the expiration of any period of reference under subsection (c) or (d) of this section, whichever is later, the Commission has not filed a civil action in a case involving a government, governmental agency, or political subdivision, or the Commission has not entered into a conciliation agreement to which the person aggrieved is a party, the Commission, or the Attorney General in a case involving a government, governmental agency, or political subdivision, shall so notify the person aggrieved and within ninety days after the giving of such notice a civil action may be brought against the respondent named in the charge (A) by the person claiming to be aggrieved or (B) if such charge was filed by a member of the Commission, by any person whom the charge alleges was aggrieved by the alleged unlawful employment practice. Upon application by the complainant and in such circumstances as the court may deem just, the court may appoint an attorney for such complainant and may authorize the commencement of the action without the payment of fees, costs, or security. Upon timely application, the court may, in its discretion, permit the Commission, or the Attorney General in a case involving a government, governmental agency, or political subdivision, to intervene in such civil action upon certification that the case is of general public importance. Upon request, the court may, in its discretion, stay further proceedings for not more than sixty days pending the termination of State or local proceedings described in subsections (c) or (d) of this section or further efforts of the Commission to obtain voluntary compliance.

(2) Whenever a charge is filed with the Commission and the Commission concludes on the basis of a preliminary investigation, that prompt judicial action is necessary to carry out the purposes of this Act, the Commission, or the Attorney General in a case involving a government, governmental agency, or political subdivision, may bring an action for appropriate temporary or preliminary relief pending final disposition of such charge. Any temporary restraining order or other order granting preliminary or temporary relief shall be issued in accordance with rule 65 of the Federal Rules of Civil Procedure. It shall be the duty of a court having jurisdiction over proceedings under this section to assign cases for hearing at the earliest practicable date and to cause such cases to be in every way expedited.

(3) Each United States district court and each United States court of a place subject to the jurisdiction of the United States shall have jurisdiction of actions brought under this title. Such an action may be brought in any judicial district in the State in which the unlawful employment practice is alleged to have been committed, in the judicial district in which the employment records relevant to such practice are maintained and administered, or in the judicial district in which the aggrieved person would have worked but for the alleged unlawful employment practice, but if the respondent is not found within any such district, such an action may be brought within the judicial district in which the respondent has his principal

office. For purposes of sections 1404 and 1406 of Title 28 of the United States Code, the judicial district in which the respondent has his principal office shall in all cases be considered a district in which the action might have been brought.

(4) It shall be the duty of the chief judge of the district (or in his absence, the acting chief judge) in which the case is pending immediately to designate a judge in such district to hear and determine the case. In the event that no judge in the district is available to hear and determine the case, the chief judge of the district, or the acting chief judge, as the case may be, shall certify this fact to the chief judge of the circuit (or in his absence, the acting chief judge) who shall then designate a district or circuit judge of the circuit to hear and determine the case.

(5) It shall be the duty of the judge designated pursuant to this subsection to assign the case for hearing at the earliest practicable date and to cause the case to be in every way expedited. If such judge has not scheduled the case for trial within one hundred and twenty days after issue has been joined, that judge may appoint a master pursuant to rule 53 of the Federal Rules of Civil Procedure.

Injunctions; appropriate affirmative action; equitable relief; accrual of back pay; reduction of back pay; limitations on judicial orders

(g)(l) If the court finds that the respondent has intentionally engaged in or is intentionally engaging in an unlawful employment practice charged in the complaint, the court may enjoin the respondent from engaging in such unlawful employment practice, and order such affirmative action as may be appropriate, which may include, but is not limited to, reinstatement or hiring of employees, with or without back pay (payable by the employer, employment agency, or labor organization, as the case may be, responsible for the unlawful employment practice), or any other equitable relief as the court deems appropriate. Back pay liability shall not accrue from a date more than two years prior to the filing of a charge with the Commission. Interim earnings or amounts earnable with reasonable diligence by the person or persons discriminated against shall operate to reduce the back pay otherwise allowable.

(2)(A) No order of the court shall require the admission or reinstatement of an individual as a member of a union, or the hiring, reinstatement, or promotion of an individual as an employee, or the payment to him of any back pay, if such individual was refused admission, suspended, or expelled, or was refused employment or advancement or was suspended or discharged for any reason other than discrimination on account of race, color, religion, sex, or national origin or in violation of section 2000e-3(a) of this title.

(B) On a claim in which an individual proves a violation under section 703(m) and a respondent demonstrates that the respondent would have taken the same action in the absence of the impermissible motivation factor, the court-

(i) may grant declaratory relief, injunctive relief (except as provided in clause (ii)), and attorney's fees and costs demonstrated to be directly attributable only to the pursuit of a claim under section 703(m); and

(ii) shall not award damages or issue an order requiring any admission, reinstatement, hiring, promotion, or payment described in subparagraph (A).
[Sec. 2000e5(g)(B) amended by Civil Rights Act of 1991, Pub. L. No. 102-166, §107, 105 Stat. 1075-76]

Provisions of sections 101 to 115 of Title 29 not applicable to civil actions for prevention of unlawful practices

(h) The provisions of sections 101 to 115 of Title 29 shall not apply with respect to civil actions brought under this section.

Proceedings by Commission to compel compliance with judicial orders

(i) In any case in which an employer, employment agency, or labor organization fails to comply with an order of a court issued in a civil action brought under this section, the Commission may commence proceedings to compel compliance with such order.

Appeals

(1) Any civil action brought under this section and any proceedings brought under subsection (i) shall be subject to appeal as provided in sections 1291 and 1292, Title 28.

Attorney's fee; liability of Commission and United States for costs

(k) In any action or proceeding under this subchapter the court, in its discretion, may allow the prevailing party, other than the Commission or the United States, a reasonable attorney's fee as part of the costs, and the Commission and the United States shall be liable for costs the same as a private person.

§200Oe-6 [§707] Civil Actions by Attorney General

Complaint

(a) Whenever the Attorney General has reasonable cause to believe that any person or group of persons is engaged in a pattern or practice of resistance to the full enjoyment of any of the rights secured by this subchapter, and that the pattern or practice is of such a nature and is intended to deny the full exercise of the rights herein described, the Attorney General may bring a civil action in the appropriate district court of the United States by filing with it a complaint (1) signed by him (or in his absence the Acting Attorney General), (2) setting forth facts pertaining to such pattern or practice, and (3) requesting such relief, including an application for a permanent or temporary injunction, restraining order or other order against the person or persons responsible for such pattern or practice, as he deems necessary to insure the full enjoyment of the rights herein described.

Jurisdiction; three-judge district Court for cases of general public importance: hearing, determination, expedition of action, review by Supreme Court; single-judge district court: hearing, determination, expedition of action

(b) The district courts of the United States shall have and shall exercise jurisdiction of proceedings instituted pursuant to this section, and in any such proceeding the Attorney General may file with the clerk of such court a request that a court of three judges be convened to hear and determine the case. Such request by the Attorney General shall be accompanied by a certificate that, in his opinion, the case is of general public importance. A copy of the certificate and request for a three-judge court shall be immediately furnished by such clerk to the chief judge of the circuit (or in his absence, the presiding circuit judge of the circuit) in which the case is pending. Upon receipt of such request it shall be the duty of the chief judge of the circuit or the presiding circuit judge, as the case may be, to designate immediately three judges in such circuit, of whom at

least one shall be a circuit judge and another of whom shall be a district judge of the court in which the proceeding was instituted, to hear and determine such case, and it shall be the duty of the judges so designated to assign the case for hearing at the earliest practicable date, to participate in the hearing and determination thereof, and to cause the case to be in every way expedited. An appeal from the final judgment of such court will lie to the Supreme Court.

In the event the Attorney General fails to file such a request in any such proceeding, it shall be the duty of the chief judge of the district (or in his absence, the acting chief judge) in which the case is pending immediately to designate a judge in such district to hear and determine the case. In the event that no judge in the district is available to hear and determine the case, the chief judge of the district, or the acting chief judge, as the case may be, shall certify this fact to the chief judge of the circuit (or in his absence, the acting chief judge) who shall then designate a district or circuit judge of the circuit to hear and determine the case.

It shall be the duty of the judge designated pursuant to this section to assign the case for hearing at the earliest practicable date and to cause the case to be in every way expedited.

Transfer of functions, etc., to Commission; effective date; prerequisite to transfer; execution of functions by Commission

(c) Effective two years after March 24, 1972, the functions of the Attorney General under this section shall be transferred to the Commission, together with such personnel, property, records, and unexpended balances of appropriations, allocations, and other funds employed, used, held, available, or to be made available in connection with such functions unless the President submits, and neither Rouse of Congress vetoes, a reorganization plan pursuant to chapter 9 of Title 5, inconsistent with the provisions of this subsection. The Commission shall carry out such functions in accordance with subsections (d) and (e) of this section.

Transfer of functions, etc., not to affect suits commenced pursuant to this section prior to date of transfer

(d) Upon the transfer of functions provided for in subsection (c) of this section, in all suits commenced pursuant to this section prior to the date of such transfer, proceedings shall continue without abatement, all court orders and decrees shall remain in effect, and the Commission shall be substituted as a party for the United States of America, the Attorney General, or the Acting Attorney General, as appropriate.

Investigation and action by Commission pursuant to filing of charge of discrimination; procedure

(e) Subsequent to March 24, 1972, the Commission shall have authority to investigate and act on a charge of a pattern or practice of discrimination, whether filed by or on behalf of a person claiming to be aggrieved or by a member of the Commission. All such actions shall be conducted in accordance with the procedures set forth in section 2000e-5 of this title.

§2000e-7. [§708] Effect on State Laws

Nothing in this subchapter shall be deemed to exempt or relieve any person from any liability, duty, penalty, or punishment provided by any present or future law of any

State or political subdivision of a State, other than any such law which purports to require or permit the doing of any act which would be an unlawful employment practice under this subchapter.

§2000e-8. [§709] Investigations

Examination and copying of evidence related to unlawful employment practices

(a) In connection with any investigation of a charge filed under section 2000e-5 of this title, the Commission or its designated representative shall at all reasonable times have access to, for the purposes of examination, and the right to copy any evidence of any person being investigated or proceeded against that relates to unlawful employment practices covered by this subchapter and is relevant to the charge under investigation.

Cooperation with State and local agencies administering State fair employment practices laws; participation in and contribution to research and other projects; utilization of services; payment in advance or reimbursement; agreements and rescission of agreement

(b) The Commission may cooperate with State and local agencies charged with the administration of State fair employment practices laws and, with the consent of such agencies, may, for the purpose of carrying out its functions and duties under this subchapter and within the limitation of funds appropriated specifically for such purpose, engage in and contribute to the cost of research and other projects of mutual interest undertaken by such agencies, and utilize the services of such agencies and their employees and, notwithstanding any other provision of law, pay by advance or reimbursement such agencies and their employees for services rendered to assist the Commission in carrying out this subchapter. In furtherance of such cooperative efforts, the Commission may enter into written agreements with such State or local agencies and such agreements may include provisions under which the Commission shall refrain from processing a charge in any cases or class of cases specified in such agreements or under which the Commission shall relieve any person or class of persons in such State or locality from requirements imposed under this section. The Commission shall rescind any such agreement whenever it determines that the agreement no longer serves the interest of effective enforcement of this subchapter.

Execution, retention, and preservation of records; reports to Commission; training program records; appropriate relief from regulation or order for undue hardship; procedure for exemption; judicial action to compel compliance

(c) Every employer, employment agency, and labor organization subject to this subchapter shall (1) make and keep such records relevant to the determinations of whether unlawful employment practices have been or are being committed, (2) preserve such records for such periods, and (3) make such reports therefrom as the

Commission shall prescribe by regulation or order, after public hearing, as reasonable, necessary, or appropriate for the enforcement of this subchapter or the regulations or orders thereunder. The Commission shall, by regulation, require each employer, labor organization, and joint labor-management committee subject to this subchapter which controls an apprenticeship or other training program to maintain such records as are reasonably necessary to carry out the purposes of this subchapter, including, but not limited to, a list of applicants who wish to participate in such program, including the chronological order in which applications were received, and to furnish to the Commission upon request, a detailed description of the manner in which persons are selected to participate in the apprenticeship or other training program. Any employer, employment agency, labor organization, or joint labor-management committee which believes that the application to it of any regulation or order issued under this section would result in undue hardship may apply to the Commission for an exemption from the application of such regulation or order, and, if such application for an exemption is denied, bring a civil action in the application of such regulation or order, and, if such application for an exemption is denied, bring a civil action in the United States district court for the district where such records are kept. If the Commission or the court, as the case may be, finds that the application of the regulation or order to the employer, employment agency, or labor organization in question would impose an undue hardship, the Commission or the court, as the case may be, may grant appropriate relief. If any person required to comply with the provisions of this subsection fails or refuses to do so, the United States district court for the district in which such person is found, resides, or transacts business, shall, upon application of the Commission, or the Attorney General in a case involving a government, governmental agency or political subdivision, have jurisdiction to issue to such person an order requiring him to comply.

Consultation and coordination between Commission and interested State and Federal agencies in prescribing recordkeeping and reporting requirements; availability of information furnished pursuant to recordkeeping and reporting requirements; conditions on availability

(d) In prescribing requirements pursuant to subsection (c) of this section, the Commission shall consult with other interested State and Federal agencies and shall endeavor to coordinate its requirements with those adopted by such agencies. The Commission shall furnish upon request and without cost to any State or local agency charged with the administration of fair employment practice law information obtained pursuant to subsection (c) of this section from any employer, employment agency, labor organization, or joint labor-management committee subject to the jurisdiction of such agency. Such information shall be furnished on condition that it not be made public by the recipient agency prior to the institution of a proceeding under State or local law involving such information. If this condition is violated by a recipient agency, the Commission may decline to honor subsequent requests pursuant to this subsection.

Prohibited disclosures; penalties

(e) It shall be unlawful for any officer or employee of the Commission to make public in any manner whatever any information obtained by the Commission pursuant to its authority under this section prior to the institution of any proceeding under this subchapter involving such information. Any officer or employee of the Commission who shall make public in any manner whatever any information in violation of this subsection shall be guilty of a misdemeanor and upon conviction thereof, shall be fined not more than $1,000, or imprisoned not more than one year.

§§2000e-9. [§710] Conduct of hearings and investigations pursuant to section 161 of Title 29

For the purpose of all hearings and investigations conducted by the Commission or its duly authorized agents or agencies, section 161 of Title 29 shall apply [§11 of the National Labor Relations Act].

§2OOOe-10. [§711] Posting of notices; penalties

(a) Every employer, employment agency, and labor organization, as the case may be, shall post and keep posted in conspicuous places upon its premises where notices to employees, applicants for employment, and members are customarily posted a notice to be prepared or approved by the Commission setting forth excerpts from or, summaries of, the pertinent to the filing of a complaint.

(b) A willful violation of this section shall be punishable by a fine of not more than $100 for each separate offense.

§200Oe-11. [§712] Veterans' special rights or preference

Nothing contained in this subchapter shall be construed to repeal or modify any Federal, State, territorial, or local law creating special rights or preference for veterans.

§2000e-12. [§713] Regulations; conformity of regulations with administrative procedure Act; reliance on interpretations and instructions of Commission

(a) The Commission shall have authority from time to time to issue, amend, or rescind suitable procedural regulations to carry out the provisions of this subchapter. Regulations issued under this section shall be in conformity with the standards and limitations of subchapter II of chapter 5 of Title 5.

(b) In any action or proceeding based on any alleged unlawful employment practice, no person shall be subject to any liability or punishment for or on account of (1) the commission by such person of an unlawful employment practice if he pleads and proves that the act or omission complained of was in good faith, in conformity with, and in reliance on any written interpretation or opinion of the Commission, or (2) the failure of such person to publish and file any information required by any provision of this subchapter if he pleads and proves that he failed to publish and file such information in good faith, in conformity with the instructions of the Commission issued under this subchapter regarding the filing of such information. Such a defense, if established, shall be a bar to the action or proceeding, notwithstanding that (A) after such act or omission, such interpretation or opinion is modified or rescinded or is determined by judicial authority to be invalid or of no legal effect, or (B) after publishing or filing the description and annual reports, such publication or filing is determined by judicial authority not to be in conformity with the requirements of this subchapter.

§2000e-13. [§714] Application to personnel of Commission of sections 111 and 1114 of Title 18; punishment for violation of section 1114 of Title 18

The provisions of sections 111 and 1114, Title 18, shall apply to officers, agents, and employees of the Commission in the performance of their official duties. Notwithstanding the provisions of sections 111 and 1114 of Title 18, whoever in violation of the provisions of section 1114 of such title kills a person while engaged in or on account of the performance of his official functions under this Act shall be punished by imprisonment for any term of years or for life.

§2000e-14. Coordination of efforts and elimination of competition among Federal departments, agencies, etc. in implementation and enforcement of equal employment opportunity legislation, orders, and policies; report to President and Congress

The Equal Employment Opportunity Commission shall have the responsibility for developing and implementing agreements, policies and practices designed to maximize effort, promote efficiency, and eliminate conflict, competition, duplication and inconsistency among the operations, functions and jurisdictions of the various departments, agencies and branches of the Federal Government responsible for the implementation and enforcement of equal employment opportunity legislation, orders, and policies. On or before October 1 of each year, the Equal Employment Opportunity Commission shall transmit to the President and to the Congress a report of its activities, together with such recommendations for legislative or administrative changes as it concludes are desirable to further promote the purposes of this section.

§2000e-15. [§716(c)] Presidential conferences; acquaintance of leadership with provisions for employment rights and obligations; plans for fair administration; membership

The President shall, as soon as feasible after July 2, 1964, convene one or more conferences for the purpose of enabling the leaders of groups whose members will be affected by this subchapter to become familiar with the rights afforded and obligations imposed by its provisions, and for the purpose of making plans which will result in the fair and effective administration of this subchapter when all of its provisions become effective. The President shall invite the participation in such conference or conferences of (1) the members of the President's Committee on Equal Employment Opportunity, (2) the members of the Commission on Civil Rights, (3) representatives of State and local agencies engaged in furthering equal employment opportunity, (4) representatives of private agencies engaged in furthering equal employment opportunity, and (5) representatives of employers, labor organizations, and employment agencies who will be subject to this subchapter.

§2000e-16. [§717] Employment by Federal Government

Discriminatory practices prohibited; employees or applicants for employment subject to coverage

(a) All personnel actions affecting employees or applicants for employment (except with regard to aliens employed outside the limits of the United States) in military departments as defined in section 102 of Title 5, in executive agencies as defined in section 105 of title 5 (including employees and applicants for employment who are paid from nonappropriated funds), in the United States Postal Service and the Postal Rate Commission, in those units of Government of the District of Columbia having positions in the competitive service, and in those units of the legislative and judicial branches of the Federal Government having positions in the competitive service, and in the Library of Congress shall be made free from any discrimination based on race, color, religion, sex, or national origin.

Enforcement powers of Commission; Issuance of rules, regulations, etc.; annual review and approval of national and regional equal employment opportunity plans; review and evaluation of equal employment opportunity programs and publication of progress reports; consultations with interested parties; compliance with rules, regulations, etc.; contents of national and regional equal employment opportunity plans; authority of Librarian of Congress

(b) Except as otherwise provided in this subsection, the Equal Employment Opportunity Commission shall have authority to enforce the provisions of subsection (a) of this section through appropriate remedies, including reinstatement or hiring of employees with or without back pay, as will effectuate the policies of this section, and shall issue such rules, regulations, orders and instructions as it deems necessary and appropriate to carry out its responsibilities under this section. The Equal Employment Opportunity Commission shall-

(1) be responsible for the annual review and approval of a national and regional equal employment opportunity plan which each department and agency and each appropriate unit referred to in subsection (a) of this section shall

submit in order to maintain an affirmative program of equal employment opportunity for all such employees and applicants for employment;

(2) be responsible for the review and evaluation of the operation of all agency equal employment opportunity programs, periodically obtaining and publishing (on at least a semiannual basis) progress reports from each such department, agency, or unit; and

(3) consult with and solicit the recommendations of interested individuals, groups, and organizations relating to equal employment opportunity.

The head of each such department, agency, or unit shall comply with such rules, regulations, orders, and instructions which shall include a provision that an employee or applicant for employment shall be notified of any final action taken on any complaint of discrimination filed by him thereunder. The plan submitted by each department, agency, and unit shall include, but not be limited to-

(1) provision for the establishment of training and education programs designed to provide a maximum opportunity for employees to advance so as to perform at their highest potential; and

(2) a description of the qualifications in terms of training and experience relating to equal employment opportunity for the principal and operating officials of

each such department, agency, or unit responsible for carrying out the equal employment opportunity program and of the allocation of personnel and resources proposed by such department, agency, or unit to carry out its equal employment opportunity program.

With respect to employment in the Library of Congress, authorities granted in this subsection to the Equal Employment Opportunity Commission shall be exercised by the Librarian of Congress.

Civil action by employee or applicant for employment for redress of grievances; time for bringing of action; head of department, agency, or unit as defendant

(c) Within ninety days of receipt of notice of final action taken by a department, agency, or unit referred to in subsection (a) of this section, or by the Equal Employment Opportunity Commission upon an appeal from a decision or order of such department, agency, or unit on a complaint of discrimination based on race, color, religion, sex, or national origin, brought pursuant to subsection (a) of this section, Executive Order 11478 or any succeeding Executive orders, or after one hundred and eighty days from the filing of the initial charge with the department, agency ,or unit or with the Equal Employment Opportunity Commission on appeal from a decision or order of such department, agency, or unit until such time as final action may be taken by a department, agency, or unit, an employee or applicant for employment, if

aggrieved by the final disposition of his complaint, may file a civil action as provided in section 2000e-5 of this title, in which civil action the head of the department, agency, or unit, as appropriate, shall be the defendant.
[Sec. 2000e-16 amended by the Civil Rights Act of 1991, Pub. L. No. 102-166, §114, 105 Stat. 1079]

Section 2000e-5(f) through (k) of this title applicable to civil actions

(d) The provisions of section 2000e-5 [§706(f) through (k)] of this title, as applicable, shall govern civil actions brought hereunder, and the same interest to compensate for delay in payment shall be available as in cases involving nonpublic parties.
[Sec. 2000e-16 amended by Civil Rights Act of 1991, Pub. L. No. 102-166, §114, 105 Stat. 1079]

Government agency or official not relieved of responsibility to assure nondiscrimination in employment or equal employment opportunity

(e) Nothing contained in this Act shall relieve any Government agency or official of its or his primary responsibility to assure nondiscrimination in employment as required by the Constitution and statutes or of its or his responsibilities under Executive Order 11478 relating to equal employment opportunity in the Federal Government.

§2000e-17. [§718] Procedure for denial, withholding, termination, or suspension of Government contract subse-

quent to acceptance by Government of affirmative action plan of employer; time of acceptance of plan

No Government contract, or portion thereof, with any employer, shall be denied, withheld, terminated, or suspended, by any agency or officer of the United States under any equal employment opportunity law or order, where such employer has an affirmative action plan which has previously been accepted by the Government for the same facility within the past twelve months without first according such employer full hearing and adjudication under the provisions of section 554 of Title 5, and the following pertinent sections: Provided, That if such employer has deviated substantially from such previously agreed to affirmative action plan, this section shall not apply: Provided further, that for the purposes of this section an affirmative action plan shall be deemed to have been accepted by the Government at the time the appropriate compliance agency has accepted such plan unless within forty-five days thereafter the Office of Federal Contract Compliance has disapproved such plan.

§118. Alternative Means of Dispute Resolution

Where appropriate and to the extent authorized by law, the use of alternative means of dispute resolution, including settlement negotiations, conciliation, facilitation, mediation, factfinding, minitrials, and arbitration, is encouraged to resolve disputes arising under the Acts or provisions of Federal law amended by this title.
[Pub. L. No. 102-166, §118, 105 Stat. 1081]

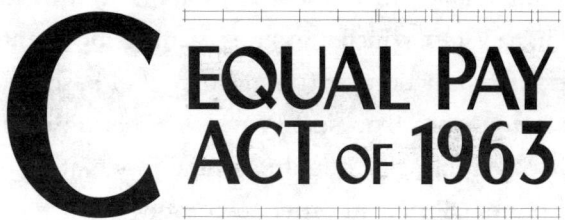

EQUAL PAY ACT OF 1963

§3 29 U.S.C. §206(d)

§206. Minimum Wage

Prohibition of sex discrimination

(d)(l) [§3] No employer having employees subject to any provisions of this section shall discriminate, within any establishment in which such employees are employed, between employees on the basis of sex by paying wages to employees in such establishment at a rate less than the rate at which he pays wages to employees of the opposite sex in such establishment for equal work on jobs the performance of which requires equal skill, effort, and responsibility, and which are performed under similar working conditions, except where such payment is made pursuant to (i) a seniority system; (ii) a merit system; (iii) a system which measures earnings by quantity or quality of production; or (iv) a differential based on any other factor other than sex: Provided, That an employer who is paying a wage rate differential in violation of this subsection shall not, in order to comply with the provisions of this subsection, reduce the wage rate of any employee.

(2) No labor organization, or its agents, representing employees of an employer having employees subject to any provisions of this section shall cause or attempt to cause such an employer to discriminate against an employee in violation of paragraph (~) of this subsection.

(3) For purposes of administration and enforcement, any amounts owing to any employee which have been withheld in violation of this subsection shall be deemed to be unpaid minimum wages or unpaid overtime compensation under this chapter.

(4) As used in this subsection, the term "labor organization" means any organization of any kind, or any agency or employee representation committee or plan, in which employees participate and which exists for the purpose, in whole or in part, of dealing with employers concerning grievances, labor disputes, wages, rates of pay, hours of employment, or conditions of work.

D 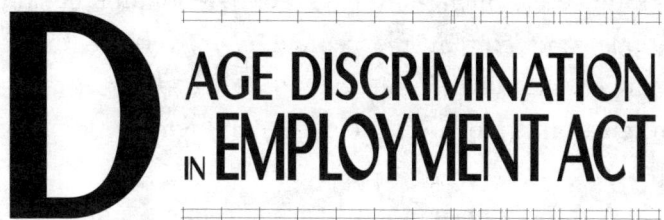 AGE DISCRIMINATION IN EMPLOYMENT ACT

29 U.S.C. Sections 621-634

Sec. 621. [Sec. 2] Congressional Statement of Findings and Purpose

(a) The Congress hereby finds and declares that-

(1) in the face of rising productivity and affluence, older workers find themselves disadvantaged in their efforts to retain employment, and especially regain employment when displaced from jobs;

(2) the setting of arbitrary age limits regardless of potential for job performance has become a common practice, and certain otherwise desirable practices may work

to the disadvantage of older persons;

(3) the incidence of unemployment, especially long-term unemployment with resultant deterioration of skill, morale, and employer acceptability is, relative to the younger ages, high among older workers; their numbers are great and growing; and their employment problems grave;

(4) the existence in industries affecting commerce, of arbitrary discrimination in employment because of age, burdens commerce and the free flow of goods in commerce.

(b) It is therefore the purpose of this chapter to promote employment of older persons based on their ability rather than age; to prohibit arbitrary age discrimination in employment; to help employers and workers find ways of meeting problems arising from the impact of age on employment.

Sec. 622. [Sec. 3] Education and Research Program; Recommendation to Congress

(a) The Secretary of Labor shall undertake studies and provide information to labor unions, management, and the general public concerning the needs and abilities of older workers, and their potentials for continued employment and contribution to the economy. In order to achieve the purposes of this chapter, the Secretary of labor shall carry on a continuing program of education and information, under which he may, among other measures-

(1) undertake research, and promote research, with a

view to reducing barriers to the employment of older persons, and the promotion of measures for utilizing their skills;

(2) publish and otherwise make available to employers, professional societies, the various media of communication, and other interested persons the finding of studies and other materials for the promotion of employment;

(3) foster through the public employment service system and through cooperative effort the development of facilities of public and private agencies for expanding the opportunities and potentials of older persons;

(4) sponsor and assist State and community informational and educational programs.

(b) Not later than six months after the effective date of this chapter, the Secretary shall recommend to the Congress any measures he may deem desirable to change the lower or upper age limits set forth in section 631 of this title.

Sec. 623. [Sec 4] Prohibition of Age Discrimination

Employer Practices

(a) It shall be unlawful for an employer-

(1) to fail or refuse to hire or to discharge an individual or otherwise discriminate against any individual with respect to his compensation, terms, conditions, or privileges of employment, because of such individual's age:

(2) to limit, segregate, or classify his employees in any way which would deprive or tend to deprive any individual of employment opportunities or otherwise adversely

affect his status as an employee, because of such individual's age; or

(3) to reduce the wage rate of any employee in order to comply with this chapter.

Employment Agency Practices

(b) It shall be unlawful for an employment agency to fail or refuse to refer for employment, or otherwise to discriminate against, any individual because of such individual's age, or to classify or refer for employment any individual on the basis of such individual's age.

Labor Organization Practices

(c) It shall be unlawful for a labor organization-

(1) to exclude or to expel from its membership, or otherwise to discriminate against, any individual because of his age;

(2) to limit, segregate, or classify its membership, or to classify or fail or refuse to refer for employment any individual, in any way which would deprive or tend to deprive any individual of employment opportunities, or would limit such employment opportunities or otherwise adversely affect his status as an employee or as an applicant for employment, because of such individual age;

(3) to cause or attempt to cause an employer to discriminate against an individual in violation of this section.

Opposition to Unlawful Practices; Participation in Investigations, Proceedings, or Litigation

(d) It shall be unlawful for an employer to discriminate against any of his employees or applicants for employment, for an employment agency to discriminate against any individual, or for a labor organization to discriminate against any individual member thereof or applicant for membership, because such individual, member or applicant for membership has opposed any practice made unlawful by this section, or because such individual, member or applicant for membership has made a charge, testified, assisted, or participated in any manner in an investigation, proceeding, or litigation under this chapter.

Printing or Publication of Notice or Advertisement Indicating Preference, Limitation, Etc.

(e) It shall be unlawful for an employer, labor organization, or employment agency to print or publish, or cause to be printed or published, any notice or advertisement relating to employment by such an employer or membership in or any classification or referral for employment by such a labor organization, or relating to any classification or referral for employment by such an employment agency, indicating any preference, limitation, specification, or discrimination, based on age.

Lawful Practices; Age as Occupational Qualification; Other Reasonable Factors; Seniority System; Employee Benefit Plans; Discharge or Discipline for Good Cause

(f) It shall not be unlawful for an employer, employment agency, or labor organization-

(1) to take any action otherwise prohibited under

subsections (a), (b), (c), or (e) of this section where age is a bona fide occupational qualification reasonably necessary to the normal operation of the particular business, or where the differentiation is based on reasonable factors other than age, or where such practices involve an employee in a workplace in a foreign country, and compliance with such subsection would cause said employer, or a corporation controlled by such employer to violate the law of the country in which said workplace is located.

(2) to take any action otherwise prohibited under subsection (a), (b), (c), or (e) of this section-

(A) to observe the terms of a bona fide seniority system that is not intended to evade the purposes of this Act, except that no such seniority system shall require or permit the involuntary retirement of any individual specified by section 12(a) because of the age of such individual; or

(B) to observe the terms of a bona fide employee benefit plan-

(i) where, for each benefit or benefit package, the actual amount of payment made or cost incurred on behalf of an older worker is no less than that made or incurred on behalf of a younger worker, as permissible under section 1625.10 title 29, Code of Federal Regulations (as in effect on June 22, 1989); or

(ii) that is a voluntary early retirement incentive plan inconsistent with the relevant purpose or purposes of this Act.

Notwithstanding clause (i) or (ii) of subparagraph (B), no such employee benefit plan or voluntary early retirement incentive plan shall excuse the failure to hire an individual, and no such employee benefit plan shall require or permit the involuntary retirement of any individual specified by section 12(a), because of the age of such individual. An employer, employment agency, or labor organization acting under subparagraph (A), or under clause (i) or (ii) of subparagraph (B), shall have the burden of proving that such actions are lawful in any civil enforcement proceeding brought under this Act; or

(3) to discharge or otherwise discipline an individual for good cause.

Entitlement to Coverage Under Group Health Plan

(g)(l) For purposes of this section, any employer must provide that any employee aged 65 or older, and any employee's spouse aged 65 or older, shall be entitled to coverage under any group health plan offered to such employees under the same conditions as any employee, and the spouse of such employee, under age 65.

(2) For purposes of paragraph (1), the term "group health plan" has the meaning given to such term in section 162(i)(2) of Title 26.

Practices of Foreign Corporations Controlled by American Employers; Foreign Persons Not Controlled by American Employers; Factors Determining Control

(h)(1) If an employer controls a corporation whose place of incorporation is in a foreign country, any practice by such corporation prohibited under this section shall be presumed to be such practice by such employer.

(2) The prohibitions of this section shall not apply where the employer is a foreign person not controlled by an American employer.

(3) For the purpose of this subsection the determination of whether an employer controls a corporation shall be based upon the-

(A) interrelation of operations;

(B) common management;

(C) centralized control of labor relations, and

(D) common ownership or financial control, of the employer and the corporation.

Firefighters and Law Enforcement Officers Attaining Hiring or Retiring Age Under State or Local law on March 3, 1983

(i) It shall not be unlawful for an employer which is a State, a political subdivision of a State, an agency or instrumentality of a State or a political subdivision of a State, or an interstate agency to fail or refuse to hire or to discharge any individual because of such individual's age if such action is taken-

(1) with respect to the employment of an individual as a firefighter or as a law enforcement officer and the individual has attained the age of hiring or retirement in effect under applicable State or local law on March 3, 1983, and

(2) pursuant to a bona fide hiring or retirement plan that is not a subterfuge to evade the purposes of this chapter.

Employee Pension Benefit Plans; Cessation or Deduction of Benefit Accrual or of Allocation to Employee Account; Distribution of Benefits After Attainment of Normal Retirement Age; Compliance; Highly Compensated Employees

(j)(1) Except as otherwise provided in this subsection, it shall be unlawful for an employer, an employment agency, a labor organization, or any combination thereof to establish or maintain an employee pension benefit plan which requires or permits-

(A) in the case of a defined benefit plan, the cessation of an employee's benefit accrual, or the reduction of the rate of an employee's benefit accrual, because of age, or

(B) in the case of a defined contribution plan, the cessation of allocations to an employee's account, or the reduction of the rate at which amounts are allocated to an employee's account, because of age.

(2) Nothing in this section shall be construed to prohibit an employer, employment agency, or labor organization from observing any provision of an employee pension benefit plan to the extent that such provision imposes (without regard to age) a limitation on the amount of benefits that the plan provides or a limitation on the number of years of service or years of participation which are taken into account for purposes of determining benefit accrual under the plan.

(3) In the case of any employee who, as of the end of any plan year under a defined benefit plan, has attained normal retirement age under such plan-

(A) if distribution of benefits under such plan with

respect to such employee has commenced as of the end of such plan year, then any requirement of this subsection for continued accrual of benefits under such plan with respect to such employee during such plan year shall be treated as satisfied to the extent of the actuarial equivalent of in-service distribution of benefits, and

(B) if distribution of benefits under such plan with respect to such employee has not commenced as of the end of such year in accordance with section 1056(a)(3) of this title and section 401(a)(14)(C) of title 26, and the payment of benefits under such plan with respect to such employee is not suspended during such plan year pursuant to section 1053(a)(3)(B) of this title or section 41 l(a)(3)(B) of title 26, then any requirement of this subsection for continued accrual of benefits under such plan with respect to such employee during such plan year shall be treated as satisfied to the extent of any adjustment in the benefit payable under the plan during such plan year attributable to the delay in the distribution of benefits after the attainment of normal retirement age.

The provision of this paragraph shall apply in accordance with regulations of the Secretary of the Treasury. Such regulations shall provide for the application of the preceding provisions of this paragraph to all employee pension benefit plans subject to this subsection and may provide for the application of such provisions, in the case of any such employee, with respect to any period of time within a plan year.

(4) Compliance with the requirements of this subsection with respect to an employee pension benefit plan

shall constitute compliance with the requirements of this subsection relating to benefit accrual under such plan.

(5) Paragraph (1) shall not apply with respect to any employee who is a highly compensated employee (within the meaning of section 414(q) of title 26) to the extent provided in regulations prescribed by the Secretary of the Treasury for purposes of precluding discrimination in favor of highly compensated employees within the meaning of subchapter D of chapter 1 of title 26.

(6) A plan shall not be treated as failing to meet the requirements of paragraph (1) solely because the subsidized portion of any early retirement benefit is disregarded in determining benefit accruals.

(7) Any regulations prescribed by the Secretary of the Treasury pursuant to clause (v) of section 411 (b)(I)(H) of title 26 and subparagraphs (C) and (D) of section 411 (b)(2) of title 26 shall apply with respect to the requirements of this subsection in the same manner and to the same extent as such regulations apply with respect to the requirements of such sections 411 (b)(1)(H) and 411 (b)(2) of title 26.

(8) A plan shall not be treated as failing to meet the requirements of this section solely because such plan provides a normal retirement age described in section 1 002(24)(B) of this title and section 411(a)(8)(B) of title 26.

(9) For purposes of this subsection-

(A) The terms "employee pension benefit plan," "defined benefit plan," "defined contribution plan," and "normal retirement age" have the meanings provided such terms in section 1002 of this title.

(B) The term "compensation" has the meaning provided by section 414(s) of title 26.

(k) A seniority system or employee benefit plan shall comply with this Act regardless of the date of adoption of such system or plan.

(1) Notwithstanding clause (i) or (ii) of subsection (f)(2)(B)-

(1) It shall not be a violation of subsection (a), (b), (c), or (e) solely because-

(A) an employee pension benefit plan 9 as defined in section 3(2) of the Employee Retirement Income Security Act of 1974 (29 U.S.C. 1002(2)) provides for the attainment of a minimum age as a condition of eligibility for normal or early retirement benefits; or

(B) as defined benefit plan (as defined in section 3(35) of such Act) provides for-

(i) payments that constitute the subsidized portion of an early retirement benefit; or

(ii) social security supplements for plan participants that commence before the age and terminate at the age (specified by the plan) when participants are eligible to receive reduced or unreduced old-age insurance benefits under title II of the Social Security Act (42 U.S.C. 401 et seq.) and that do not exceed such old-age insurance benefits.

(2)(A) It shall not be a violation of subsection (a), (b), (c), or (e) solely because following a contingent event unrelated to age-

(i) the value of any retiree health benefits received by an individual eligible for an immediate pension; and

(ii) the value of any additional pension benefits that

are made available solely as a result of the contingent event unrelated to age and following which the individual is eligible for not less than an immediate and unreduced pension, are deducted from severance pay made available as a result of the contingent event unrelated to age.

(B) For an individual who receives immediate pension benefits that are actuarially reduced under subparagraph (A(i) shall be reduced by the same percentage as the reduction in the pension benefits.

(C) For purposes of this paragraph, severance pay shall include that portion of supplemental unemployment compensation benefits (as described in section 501 (c)(17) of the Internal Revenue Code of 1986) that-

(i) constitutes additional benefits of up to 52 weeks;

(ii) has the primary purpose and effect of continuing benefits until an individual becomes eligible for an immediate and unreduced pension; and

(iii) is discontinued once the individual becomes eligible for an immediate and unreduced pension.

(D) For purposes of this paragraph, the term "retiree health benefits" means benefits provided pursuant to a group health plan covering retirees, for which (determined as of the contingent event unrelated to age-

(i) the package of benefits provided by the employer for the retirees who are below the age 65 is at least comparable to benefits provided under title XVIII of the Social Security Act (42 U.S.C. 1395 et seq.); and

(ii) the package of benefits provided by the employer for the retirees who are age 65 and above is at least comparable to that offered under a plan that provides a benefit package with one-fourth the value of benefits provided under title XVIII of such Act.

(E)(i) If the obligation of the employer to provide retiree health benefits is of limited duration, the value for each individual shall be calculated at a rate of $3,000 per year for benefit years before age 65, and $750 per year for benefit year beginning at age 65 and above.

(ii) If the obligation of the employer to provide retiree health benefits is of limited duration, the value for each individual shall be calculated at a rate of $48,000 for individuals below age 65, and $24,000 for individuals age 65 and above.

(iii) The values described in clauses (i) and (ii) shall be calculated based on the age of the individual as of the date of the contingent event unrelated to age. The values are effective on the date of enactment of this subsection, and shall be adjusted on an annual basis, with respect to a contingent event that occurs subsequent to the first year after the date of enactment of this subsection, based on the medical component of the Consumer Price Index for all-urban consumers published by the Department of Labor.

(iv) If an individual is required to pay a premium for retiree health benefits, the value calculated pursuant to this subparagraph shall be reduced by whatever percentage of the overall premium the individual is required to pay.

(f) If an employer that has implemented a deduction pursuant to subparagraph (A) fails to fulfill the obligation described in subparagraph (E), any aggrieved individual may bring an action for specific performance of the obligation described in subparagraph (E). The relief shall be in addition to any other remedies provided under Federal or State law.

(3) It shall not be a violation of subsection (a), (b), (c), or (e) solely because an employer provides a bona fide employee benefit plan or plans under which long term disability benefits received by an individual are reduced by any pension benefits (other than those attributable to employee contributions)-

(A) paid to the individual that the individual voluntarily elects to receive; or

(B) for which an individual who has attained the later of age 62 or normal retirement age is eligible.

Sec. 624. [Sec. 5] Study by Secretary of Labor

(a)(1) The Secretary of Labor is directed to undertake an appropriate study of institutional and other arrangements giving rise to involuntary retirement, and report his finding and any appropriate legislative recommendations to the President and to the Congress. Such study shall include-

(A) an examination of the effect of the amendment made by section 3(a) of the Age Discrimination in Employment Act Amendments of 1978 [amending 29 U.S.C. sec. 63l] in raising the upper age limitation established by section 12(a) of this Act [29 U.S.C. sec. 631(a)] to 70 years of age;

(B) a determination of the feasibility of eliminating such limitation;

(C) a determination of the feasibility of raising such limitation above 70 years of age; and

(D) an examination of the effect of the exemption contained in section 12(c) [29 U.S.C. sec. 631(c)], relating to tenured teaching personnel.

(2) The Secretary may undertake the study required by paragraph (1) of this subsection directly or by contract or other arrangement.

(b) The report required by subsection (a) of this section shall be transmitted to the President and to the Congress as an interim report not later than January 1, 1981, and in final form not later than January 1, 1982.

Sec. 625. [Sec. 6] Administration

The Secretary shall have the power-

Delegation of Functions; Appointment of Personnel; Technical Assistance

(a) to make delegations, to appoint such agents and employees, and to pay for technical assistance on a fee for service basis, as he deems necessary to assist him in the performance of his functions under this chapter.

Cooperation with Other Agencies, Employers, Labor Organizations, and Employment Agencies

(b) to cooperate with regional, State, local, and other agencies, and to cooperate with and furnish technical assistance to employers, labor organizations, and employment agencies to aid in effectuating the purposes of this chapter.

Sec. 626. [Sec. 7] Recordkeeping, Investigation, and Enforcement

(a) The Secretary shall have the power to make investigations and require the keeping of records necessary or appropriate for the administration of this chapter in accordance with the powers and procedures provided in sections 209 and 211 of this title.

Enforcement; Prohibition of Age Discrimination Under Fair labor Standards; Unpaid Minimum Wages and Unpaid Overtime Compensation; Liquidated Damages; Judicial Relief; Conciliation, Conference, and Persuasion

(b) The provisions of this chapter shall be enforced in accordance with the powers, remedies, and procedures provided in sections 211(b), 216 (except for subsection (a) thereof), and 217 of this title, and subsection (c) of this section. Any act prohibited under section 623 of this title shall be deemed to be a prohibited act under section 215 of this title. Amounts owing to a person as a result of a violation of this chapter shall be deemed to be unpaid minimum wages or unpaid over time compensation for purposes of sections 216 and 217 of this title: Provided, That liquidated damages shall be payable only in cases of willful violations of this chapter. In any action brought to enforce this chapter the court shall have jurisdiction to grant such legal or equitable relief as may be appropriate to effectuate the purposes of this chapter, including without limitation judgments compelling employment, reinstatement or promotion, or enforcing the liability for amounts deemed to be unpaid minimum wages or unpaid over time compensation under this section. Before instituting any action under this section, the Secretary shall attempt to eliminate the discriminatory practice or practices alleged, and to effect voluntary compliance with the requirements of this chapter through informal methods of conciliation, conference, and persuasion.

Civil Actions; Persons Aggrieved; Jurisdiction; Judicial Relief; Termination of Individual Action upon Commencement of Action by Secretary

(c)(I) Any person aggrieved may bring a civil action in any court of competent jurisdiction for such legal or equitable relief as will effectuate the purposes of this chapter: Provided, That the right of any person to bring such action shall terminate upon the commencement of an action by the Secretary to enforce the right of such employee under this chapter.

(2) In an action brought under paragraph (I), a person shall be entitled to a trial by jury of any issue of fact in any such action for recovery of amounts owing as a result of a violation of this Act, regardless of whether equitable relief is sought by any party in such action.

Civil Actions; Notice to Secretary; Timeliness; Conciliation, Conference, and Persuasion

(d) No civil action may be commenced by an individual under this section until 60 days after a charge alleging unlawful discrimination has been filed with the Secretary. Such a charge shall be filed-

(1) within 180 days after the alleged unlawful practice occurred; or

(2) in a case to which section 633(b) of this title applies, within 300 days after the alleged unlawful practice occurred, or within 30 after the receipt by the individual of notice of termination of proceeding under State law, whichever is earlier. Upon receiving such a charge, the Secretary shall promptly notify all persons named in such charge as prospective defendants in the action and shall promptly seek to eliminate any alleged unlawful practice by informal methods of conciliation, conference, and persuasion.

Statute of Limitations; Reliance in Future on Administrative
Rulings, Etc.

Section 259 of this title shall apply to actions under this chapter. [f a charge filed with the Commission under this chapter is dismissed or the proceedings of the Commission are otherwise terminated by the Commission, the Commission shall notify the person aggrieved. A civil action may be brought under this section by a person defined in section 630(a) of this title against the respondent named in the charge within 90 days after the date of the receipt of such notice.

Sec. 627. [Sec. 8] Notices to Be Posted

Every employer, employment agency, and labor organization shall post and keep posted in conspicuous places upon its premises a notice to be prepared or approved by the Secretary setting forth information as the Secretary deems appropriate to effectuate the purposes of this chapter.

Sec. 628. [Sec. 9] Rules and Regulations; Exemptions

In accordance with the provisions of subchapter II of chapter 5 of Title 5, the Secretary of Labor may issue such rules and regulations as he may consider necessary or appropriate for carrying out this chapter, and may establish such reasonable exemptions to and from any or all provisions of this chapter as he may find necessary and proper in the public interest.

Sec. 629. [Sec. 10] Criminal Penalties

Whoever shall forcibly resist, oppose, impede, intimidate or interfere with a duly authorized representative of the Secretary while he is engaged in the performance of duties under this chapter shall be punished by a fine of not more than $500 or by imprisonment for not more than one year, or by both: Provided, however that no person shall be imprisoned under this section except when there has been a prior conviction hereunder.

Sec. 630. [Sec. 11] Definitions

For purposes of this chapter—

(a) The term "person" means one or more individuals, partner- ships, associations, labor organizations, corporations, business trusts, legal representatives, or any organized groups of persons.

(b) The term "employer" means a person engaged in an industry affecting commerce who has twenty or more employees for each working day in each of twenty or more calendar weeks in the current or preceding calendar year: Provided, That prior to June 30, 1968, employers having fewer than fifty employees shall not be considered employers. The term also means (1) any agent of such a person, and (2) a State or political subdivision of a State and any agency or instrumentality of a State or political subdivision of a State, and any interstate agency, but such term does not include the United States, or a corporation wholly owned by the Government of the United States.

(c) The term "employment agency" means any person regularly undertaking with or without compensation to procure employees for an employer and includes an agent to such a person; but shall not include an agency of the United States.

(d) The term "labor organization" means a labor organization engaged in an industry affecting commerce, and any agent of such an organization, and includes any organization of any kind, any agency, or employee representation committee, group association, or plan so engaged in which employees participate and which exists for the purpose, in whole or in part, of dealing with employers concerning grievances, labor disputes, wages, rates of pay, hours, or other terms or conditions of employment, and any conference, general committee, joint or system board, or joint council so engaged which is subordinate to a nation or international labor organization.

(e) A labor organization shall be deemed to be engaged in an industry affecting commerce if (1) it maintains or operates a hiring hall or hiring office which procures employees for an employer or procures for employees opportunities to work for an employer, or (2) the number of its members (or, where it is a labor organization composed of other labor organizations or their representatives, if the aggregate number of the members of such other labor organization) is fifty or more prior to July 1, 1968, or twenty-five or more on or after July 1, 1968, and such labor organization-

(1) is the certified representative of employees under the provisions of the National Labor Relations Act, as amended, or the Railway Labor Act, as amended; or

(2) although not certified, is a national or international labor organization or a local labor organization recognized or acting as the representative of employees of an employer or employers engaged in an industry affecting commerce; or

(3) has chartered a local labor organization or subsidiary body which is representing or actively seeking to represent employees of employers within the meaning of paragraph (1) or (2); or

(4) has been chartered by a labor organization repre-

senting or actively seeking to represent employees within the meaning or paragraph (1) or (2) as the local or subordinate body through which such employees may enjoy membership or become affiliated with such labor organization; or

(5) is a conference, general committee, joint or system board, or joint council subordinate to a national or international labor organization, which includes a labor organization engaged in industry affecting commerce within the meaning of any of the preceding paragraphs of this subsection.

(f) The term "employee" means an individual employed by any employer except that the term "employee" shall not include any person elected to public office in any State or political subdivision of any State by the qualified voters thereof, or any person chosen by such officer to be on such officer's personal staff, or an appointee to the policymaking level or an immediate adviser with respect to the exercise of the constitutional or legal powers of the office. The exemption set forth in the preceding sentence shall not include employees subject to the civil service laws of a State government, governmental agency, or political subdivision. The term "employee" includes an individual who is a citizen of the United States employed by an employer in a work place in a foreign country.

(g) The term "commerce" means trade, traffic, commerce, transportation, transmission, or communication among the several States; or between a State and any place outside thereof; or within the District of Columbia, or a possession of the United States; or between points in the same State but through a point outside thereof.

(h) The term "industry affecting commerce" means any activity, business, or industry in commerce or in which a labor dispute would hinder or obstruct commerce or the free flow of commerce and includes any activity or industry "affecting commerce" within the meaning of the Labor-Management Reporting and Disclosure Act of 1959.

(i) The term "State" includes a State of the United States, the District of Columbia, Puerto Rico, the Virgin Islands, American
Samoa, Guam, Wake Island, The Canal Zone, and Outer Continental
Shelf Islands defined in the Outer Continental Shelf Islands Act.

(j) The term "firefighter" means an employee, the duties of whose position are primarily to perform work directly connected with the control and extinguishment of fires or the maintenance and use of firefighting apparatus and equipment, including an employee engaged in this activity who is transferred to a supervisory or administrative position.

(k) The term "law enforcement officer" means an employee, the duties of whose position are primarily the investigation, apprehension, or detention of individual suspected or convicted of offenses against the criminal laws of a State, including an employee engaged in this activity who is transferred to a supervisory or administrative position. For the purpose of this subsection, "detention" includes the duties of employees assigned to guard individuals incarcerated in any penal institution.

(l) The term "compensation, terms, conditions, or privileges of employment" encompasses all employee benefits, including such benefits provided pursuant to a bona fide employee benefit plan.

Sec. 631. [Sec. 12] Age Limits

(a) The prohibitions in this chapter (except the provisions of section 623(g) of this title) shall be limited to individuals who are at least 40 years of age.

(b) In the case of any personnel action affecting employees or applicants for employment which is subject to the provisions of section 633a of this title, the prohibitions established in section 633(a) of this title shall be limited to individuals who are at least 40 years of age.

(c)(1) Nothing in this chapter shall be construed to prohibit compulsory retirement of any employee who has attained 65 years of age but not 70 years of age, and who, for the 2-year period immediately before retirement, is employed in a bona fide executive or a high policymaking position, if such employee is entitled to an immediate nonforfeitable annual retirement benefit from a pension, profit-sharing savings, or deferred compensation plan, or any combination of such plans, of the employer of such employee, which equals, in the aggregate, at least $44,000.

(2) In applying the retirement benefit test of paragraph (1) of this subsection, if any such retirement benefit is in a form other than a straight life annuity (with no ancillary benefits), or if employees contribute to any such plan or make rollover contributions, such benefit shall be

adjusted in accordance with regulations prescribed by the Secretary, after consultation with the Secretary of the Treasury, so that the benefit is the equivalent of a straight life annuity (with no ancillary benefits) under a plan to which employees do not contribute and under which no rollover contributions are made.

Sec. 632. [Sec. 13] Annual Report to Congress

The Secretary shall submit annually in January a report to the Congress covering his activities for the preceding year and including such information, data, and recommendations for further legislation in connection with the matters covered by this chapter as he may find advisable. Such report shall contain an evaluation and appraisal by the Secretary of the effect of the minimum and maximum ages established by this chapter, together with his recommendations to the Congress.

In making such evaluation and appraisal, the Secretary shall take into consideration any changes which may have occurred in the general age level of the population, the effect of the chapter upon workers not covered by its provisions, and such other factors as he may deem pertinent.

Sec. 633. [Sec. 14] Federal-State Relationship

Federal Action Superseding State Action

(a) Nothing in this chapter shall affect the jurisdiction of any agency of any State performing like functions with regard to discriminatory employment practices on account of age except that upon commencement of action under this chapter such action shall supersede any State action.

Limitation of Federal Action upon Commencement of State Proceedings

(b) In the case of an alleged unlawful practice occurring in a State which has a law prohibiting discrimination in employment because of age and establishing or authorizing a State authority to grant or seek relief from such discriminatory practice, no suit may be brought under section 626 of this title before the expiration of sixty days after proceedings have been commenced under the State law, unless such proceedings have been earlier terminated: Provided, That such sixty-day period shall be extended to one hundred and twenty days during the first year after the effective date of such State law. If any requirement for the commencement of such proceedings is imposed by a State authority other than a requirement of the filing of a written and signed statement of the facts upon which the proceeding is based, the proceeding shall be deemed to have been commenced for the purposes of this subsection at the time such statement is sent by registered mail to the appropriate State authority.

Sec. 633a. [Sec. 15] Nondiscrimination on Account of Age in Federal Government Employment

Federal Agencies Affected

(a) All personnel actions affecting employees or applicants for employment who are at least 40 years of age (except with regard to aliens employed outside the limits of the United States) in military departments as defined in section 102 of Title 5, in executive agencies as defined in section 105 of Title 5 (including employees and applicants for employment who are paid from nonappropriated funds), in the United States Postal Service and the Postal Rate Commission, in those units in the government of the District of Columbia having positions in the competitive service, and in those units of the legislative and judicial branches of the Federal Government having positions in the competitive service, and in the Library of Congress shall be made free from any discrimination based on age.

Enforcement by Civil Service Commission and by Librarian of Congress in Library of Congress; Remedies; Rules, Regulations, Orders and Instruction of Commission; Compliance by Federal Agencies; Powers and Duties of Commission; Notification of Final Action on Complaint of Discrimination; Exemptions: Bona Fide Occupational Qualification

(b) Except as otherwise provided in this subsection, the Civil Service Commission is authorized to enforce the provisions of subsection (a) of this section through appropriate remedies, including reinstatement of hiring of employees with or without backpay, as will effectuate the policies of this section. The Civil Service Commission shall issue such rules, regulations, orders, and instructions as it deems necessary and appropriate to carry out its responsibilities under this section. The Civil Service Commission shall-

(1) be responsible for the review and evaluation of the operation of all agency programs designed to carry out the policy of this section, periodically obtaining and publishing (on at least a semiannual basis) progress reports from each department, agency, or unit referred to in subsection (a) of this section;

(2) consult with and solicit the recommendations of interested individuals, groups, and organizations relating to nondiscrimination in employment on account of age; and

(3) provide for the acceptance and processing of complaints of discrimination in Federal employment on account of age.

The head of each such department, agency, or unit shall comply with such rules, regulations, orders, and instructions of the Civil Service Commission which shall include a provision that an employee or applicant for employment shall be notified of any final action taken on any complaint of discrimination filed by him thereunder. Reasonable exemptions to the provisions of this section may be established by the Commission but only when the Commission has established a maximum age requirement on the basis of a determination that age is a bona fide occupational qualification necessary to the performance of the duties of the position. With respect to employment in the Library of Congress, authorities granted in this subsection to the Civil Service Commission shall be exercised by the Librarian of Congress.

Civil Actions; Jurisdiction; Relief

(c) Any person aggrieved may bring a civil action in any Federal district court of competent jurisdiction for such legal or equitable relief as will effectuate the purposes of this chapter.

Same; Notice to Commission; Time of Notice; Commission Notification of Prospective Defendants; Commission Elimination of Unlawful Practices

(d) When the individual has not filed a complaint concerning age discrimination with the Commission, no civil action may be commenced by any individual under this section until the individual has given the Commission not less than thirty days' notice of an intent to file such action. Such notice shall be filed within one hundred and eighty days after the alleged unlawful practice occurred. Upon receiving a notice of intent to sue, the Commission shall promptly notify all persons named therein as prospective defendants in the action and take any appropriate action to assure the elimination of any unlawful practice.

Duty of Government Agency or Official

(e) Nothing contained in this section shall relieve any

Government agency or official of the responsibility to assure nondiscrimination on account of age in employment as required under any provision of Federal law.

Applicability of Statutory Provisions to Personnel Action of Federal Department, Etc.

(f) Any personnel action of any department, agency, or other entity referred to in subsection (a) of this section shall not be subject to, or affected by, any provision of this chapter, other than the provisions of section 631(b) of this title and the provisions of this section.

FAMILY AND MEDICAL LEAVE ACT

29 U.S.C. §§ 2601 et seq.

§ 2601. Findings and purposes

(a) **Findings.** Congress finds that-

(1) the number of single-parent households and two-parent households in which the single parent or both parents work is increasing significantly;

(2) it is important for the development of children and the family unit that fathers and mothers be able to participate in early childrearing and the care of family members who have serious health conditions;

(3) the lack of employment policies to accommodate

working parents can force individuals to choose between job security and parenting;

(4) there is inadequate job security for employees who have serious health conditions that prevent them from working for temporary periods;

(5) due to the nature of the roles of men and women in our society, the primary responsibility for family caretaking often falls on women, and such responsibility affects the working lives of women more than it affects the working lives of men; and

(6) employment standards that apply to one gender only have serious potential for encouraging employers to discriminate against employees and applicants for employment who are of that gender.

(b) Purposes. It is the purpose of this Act—

(1) to balance the demands of the workplace with the needs of families, to promote the stability and economic security of families, and to promote national interests in preserving family integrity;

(2) to entitle employees to take reasonable leave for medical reasons for the birth or adoption of a child, and for the care of a child, spouse, or parent who has a serious health condition;

(3) to accomplish the purposes described in paragraphs (1) and (2) in a manner that accommodates the legitimate interests of employers;

(4) to accomplish the purposes described in paragraphs (1) and (2) in a manner that, consistent with the Equal Protection Clause of the Fourteenth Amendment [U.S.C., Constitution, Amendment 14, § 1] minimizes the

potential for employment discrimination on the basis of sex by ensuring generally that leave is available for eligible medical reasons (including maternity-related disability) and for compelling family reasons, on a gender-neutral basis; and

(5) to promote the goal of equal employment opportunity for women and men, pursuant to such clause.

GENERAL REQUIREMENTS FOR LEAVE

§ 2611. Definitions

As used in this title [29 U.S.C. §§ 2611 et seq.]:

(1) Commerce. The terms "commerce" and 'industry or activity affecting commerce" mean any activity, business, or industry in commerce or in which a labor dispute would hinder or obstruct commerce or the free flow of commerce, and include "commerce" and any "industry affecting commerce", as defined in paragraphs (1) and (3) of section 501 of the Labor Management Relations Act, 1947 (29 U.S.C. 142 (1) and (3)).

(2) Eligible employee. (A) In general. The term "eligible employee" means an employee who has been employed-

(i) for at least 12 months by the employer with respect to whom leave is requested under section 102 [29 U.S.C. § 2612]; and

(ii) for at least 1,250 hours of service with such employer during the previous 12-month period.

(B) Exclusions. The term "eligible employee" does not

include

(i) any Federal officer or employee covered under subchapter V of chapter 63 of title 5, United States Code [5 U.S.C. §§ 6381 et seq.] (as added by Title II of this Act); or

(ii) any employee of an employer who is employed at a worksite at which such employer employs less than 50 employees if the total number of employees employed by that employer within 75 miles of that worksite is less than 50.

(C) Determination. For purposes of determining whether an employee meets the hours of service requirement specified in subparagraph (A)(ii), the legal standards established under section 7 of the Fair Labor Standards Act of 1938 (29 U.S.C. 207) shall apply.

(8) Employ; employee; State. The terms "employ", "employee", and "State" have the same meanings given such terms in subsections (c), (e), and (g) of section 3 of the Fair Labor Standards Act of 1938 (29 U.S.C. 203(c), (e), and (g)).

(4) Employer. (A) In general. The term "employer"-

(i) means any person engaged in commerce or in any industry or activity affecting commerce who employs 50 or more employees for each working day during each of 20 or more calendar workweeks in the current or preceding calendar year;

(ii) includes-

(I) any person who acts, directly or indirectly, in the interest of an employer to any of the employees of such employer; and

(II) any successor in interest of an employer; and

(iii) includes any "public agency", as defined in section 3(x) of the Fair Labor Standards Act of 1938 (29 U.S.C. 203(x)).

(B) Public agency. For purposes of subparagraph (A)(iii), a public agency shall be considered to be a person engaged in commerce or in an industry or activity affecting commerce.

(5) Employment benefits. The term "employment benefits" means all benefits provided or made available to employees by an employer, including group life insurance, health insurance, disability insurance, sick leave, annual leave, educational benefits, and pensions, regardless of whether such benefits are provided by a practice or written policy of an employer or through an "employee benefit plan", as defined in section 3(3) of the Employee Retirement Income Security Act of 1974 (29 U.S.C. 1002(3)).

(6) Health care provider. The term "health care provider" means-

(A) a doctor of medicine or osteopathy who is authorized to practice medicine or surgery (as appropriate) by the State in which the doctor practices; or

(B) any other person determined by the Secretary to be capable of providing health care services.

(7) Parent. The term "parent" means the biological parent of an employee or an individual who stood in loco parentis to an employee when the employee was a son or daughter.

(8) Person. The term "person" has the same meaning given such term in section 3(a) of the Fair Labor Standards

Act of 1938 (29 U.S.C. 203(a)).

(9) Reduced leave schedule. The term "reduced leave schedule" means a leave schedule that reduces the usual number of hours per workweek, or hours per workday, of an employee.

(10) Secretary. The term "Secretary" means the Secretary of Labor.

(11) Serious health condition. The term "serious health condition" means an illness, injury, impairment, or physical or mental condition that involves-

(A) inpatient care in a hospital, hospice, or residential medical care facility; or

(B) continuing treatment by a health care provider.

(12) Son or daughter. The term "son or daughter" means a biological, adopted, or foster child, a stepchild, a legal ward, or a child of a person standing in loco parentis, who is-

(A) under 18 years of age; or

(B) 18 years of age or older and incapable of self-care because of a mental or physical disability.

(13) Spouse. The term "spouse" means a husband or wife, as the case may be.

§ 2612. Leave requirement

(a) In general. (1) Entitlement to leave. Subject to section 103 [29 U.S.C. § 2613], an eligible employee shall be entitled to a total of 12 workweeks of leave during any 12-month period for one or more of the following:

(A) Because of the birth of a son or daughter of the

employee and in order to care for such son or daughter.

(B) Because of the placement of a son or daughter with the employee for adoption or foster care.

(C) In order to care for the spouse, or a son, daughter, or parent, of the employee, if such spouse, son, daughter, or parent has a serious health condition.

(D) Because of a serious health condition that makes the employee unable to perform the functions of the position of such employee.

(2) Expiration of entitlement. The entitlement to leave under subparagraphs (A) and (B) of paragraph (1) for a birth or placement of a son or daughter shall expire at the end of the 12-month period beginning on the date of such birth or placement.

(b) Leave taken intermittently or on a reduced leave schedule.

(1) In general. Leave under subparagraph (A) or (B) of subsection (a)(1) shall not be taken by an employee intermittently or on a reduced leave schedule unless the employee and the employer of the employee agree otherwise. Subject to paragraph (2), subsection (e)(2), and section 103(b)(5) [29 U.S.C. § 2613(b)(5)], leave under subparagraph (C) or (D) of subsection (a)(1) may be taken intermittently or on a reduced leave schedule when medically necessary. The taking of leave intermittently or on a reduced leave schedule pursuant to this paragraph shall not result in a reduction in the total amount of leave to which the employee is entitled under subsection (a) beyond the amount of leave actually taken.

(2) Alternative position. If an employee requests

intermittent leave, or leave on a reduced leave schedule, under subparagraph (C) or (D) of subsection (a)(1), that is foreseeable based on planned medical treatment, the employer may require such employee to transfer temporarily to an available alternative position offered by the employer for which the employee is qualified and that-

(A) has equivalent pay and benefits; and

(B) better accommodates recurring periods of leave than the regular employment position of the employee.

(c) Unpaid leave permitted. Except as provided in subsection (d), leave granted under subsection (a) may consist of unpaid leave. Where an employee is otherwise exempt under regulations issued by the Secretary pursuant to section 13(a)(1) of the Fair Labor Standards Act of 1938 (29 U.S.C. 213(a)(1)), the compliance of an employer with this title [29 U.S.C. §§ 2611 et seq.] by providing unpaid leave shall not affect the exempt status of the employee under such section.

(d) Relationship to paid leave. (1) Unpaid leave. If an employer provides paid leave for fewer than 12 workweeks, the additional weeks of leave necessary to attain the 12 workweeks of leave required under this title [29 U.S.C. §§ 2611 et seq.] may be provided without compensation.

(2) Substitution of paid leave. (A) In general. An eligible employee may elect, or an employer may require the employee, to substitute any of the accrued paid vacation leave, personal leave, or family leave of the employee for leave provided under subparagraph (A), (B), or (C) of subsection (a)(1) for any part of the 12-week period of such

leave under such subsection.

(B) Serious health condition. An eligible employee may elect, or an employer may require the employee, to substitute any of the accrued paid vacation leave, personal leave, or medical or sick leave of the employee for leave provided under subparagraph (C) or (D) of subsection (a)(1) for any part of the 12-week period of such leave under such subsection, except that nothing in this title [29 U.S.C. §§ 2611 et seq.] shall require an employer to provide paid sick leave or paid medical leave in any situation in which such employer would not normally provide any such paid leave.

(e) Foreseeable leave. (1) Requirement of notice. In any case in which the necessity for leave under subparagraph (A) or (B) of subsection (a)(1) is foreseeable based on an expected birth or placement, the employee shall provide the employer with not less than 30 days' notice, before the date the leave is to begin, of the employee's intention to take leave under such subparagraph, except that if the date of the birth or placement requires leave to begin in less than 30 days, the employee shall provide such notice as is practicable.

(2) Duties of employee. In any case in which the necessity for leave under subparagraph (C) or (D) of subsection (a)(1) is foreseeable based on planned medical treatment, the employee-

(A) shall make a reasonable effort to schedule the treatment so as not to disrupt unduly the operations of the employer, subject to the approval of the health care provider of the employee or the health care provider of the son, daughter, spouse, or parent of the employee, as appropriate; and

(B) shall provide the employer with not less than 30 days' notice, before the date the leave is to begin, of the employee's intention to take leave under such subparagraph, except that if the date of the treatment requires leave to begin in less than 30 days, the employee shall provide such notice as is practicable.

(f) Spouses employed by the same employer. In any case in which a husband and wife entitled to leave under subsection (a) are employed by the same employer, the aggregate number of work- weeks of leave to which both may be entitled may be limited to 12 workweeks during any 12-month period, if such leave is taken-

(1) under subparagraph (A) or (B) of subsection (a)(1); or

(2) to care for a sick parent under subparagraph (C) of such subsection.

§ 2613. Certification

(a) In general. An employer may require that a request for leave under subparagraph (C) or (D) of section 102(a)(1) [29 U.S.C. § 2612(a)] be supported by a certification issued by the health care provider of the eligible employee or of the son, daughter, spouse, or parent of the employee, as appropriate. The employee shall provide, in a timely manner, a copy of such certification to the employer.

(b) Sufficient certification. Certification provided under subsection (a) shall be sufficient if it states-

(1) the date on which the serious health condition commenced;

(2) the probable duration of the condition;

(3) the appropriate medical facts within the knowledge of the health care provider regarding the condition;

(4)(A) for purposes of leave under section 102(a)(1)(C) [29 U.S.C. § 2612(a)(1)(C)], a statement that the eligible employee is needed to care for the son, daughter, spouse, or parent and an estimate of the amount of time that such employee is needed to care for the son, daughter, spouse, or parent; and

(B) for purposes of leave under section 102(a)(1)(D) [29 U.S.C. § 2612(a)(1)(D)], a statement that the employee is unable to perform the functions of the position of the employee;

(5) in the case of certification for intermittent leave, or leave on a reduced leave schedule, for planned medical treatment, the dates on which such treatment is expected to be given and the duration of such treatment;

(6) in the case of certification for intermittent leave, or leave on a reduced leave schedule, under section 102(a)(1)(D) [29 U.S.C. § 2612(a)(1)(D)], a statement of the medical necessity for the intermittent leave or leave on a reduced leave schedule, and the expected duration of the intermittent leave or reduced leave schedule; and

(7) in the case of certification for intermittent leave, or leave on a reduced leave schedule, under section 102(a)(1)(C) [29 U.S.C. § 2612(a)(1)(C)], a statement that the employee's intermittent leave or leave on a reduced leave schedule is necessary for the care of the son, daugh-

ter, parent, or spouse who has a serious health condition, or will assist in their recovery, and the expected duration and schedule of the intermittent leave or reduced leave schedule.

(c) Second opinion. (1) In general. In any case in which the employer has reason to doubt the validity of the certification provided under subsection (a) for leave under subparagraph (C) or (D) of section 102(a)(1) [29 U.S.C. § 2612(a)(1)(C) or (D)], the employer may require, at the expense of the employer, that the eligible employee obtain the opinion of a second health care provider designated or approved by the employer concerning any information certified under subsection (b) for such leave.

(2) Limitation. A health care provider designated or approved under paragraph (1) shall not be employed on a regular basis by the employer.

(d) Resolution of conflicting opinions. (1) In general. In any case in which the second opinion described in subsection (c) differs from the opinion in the original certification provided under subsection (a), the employer may require, at the expense of the employer, that the employee obtain the opinion of a third health care provider designated or approved jointly by the employer and the employee concerning the information certified under subsection (b).

(2) Finality. The opinion of the third health care provider concerning the information certified under subsection (b) shall be considered to be final and shall be binding on the employer and the employee.

(e) Subsequent recertification. The employer may

require that the eligible employee obtain subsequent recertifications on a reasonable basis.

§ 2614. Employment and benefits protection

(a) Restoration to position. (1) In general. Except as provided in subsection (b), any eligible employee who takes leave under section 102 [29 U.S.C. § 2612] for the intended purpose of the leave shall be entitled, on return from such leave-

(A) to be restored by the employer to the position of employment held by the employee when the leave commenced; or

(B) to be restored to an equivalent position with equivalent employment benefits, pay, and other terms and conditions of employment.

(2) Loss of benefits. The taking of leave under section 102 [29 U.S.C. § 2612] shall not result in the loss of any employment benefit accrued prior to the date on which the leave commenced.

(3) Limitations. Nothing in this section shall be construed to entitle any restored employee to-

(A) the accrual of any seniority or employment benefits during any period of leave; or

(B) any right, benefit, or position of employment other than any right, benefit, or position to which the employee would have been entitled had the employee not taken the leave.

(4) Certification. As a condition of restoration under paragraph (1) for an employee who has taken leave under

section 102(a)(1)(D) [29 U.S.C. § 2612(a)(1)(D)], the employer may have a uniformly applied practice or policy that requires each such employee to receive certification from the health care provider of the employee that the employee is able to resume work, except that nothing in this paragraph shall supersede a valid State or local law or a collective bargaining agreement that governs the return to work of such employees.

(5) Construction. Nothing in this subsection shall be construed to prohibit an employer from requiring an employee on leave under section 102 [29 U.S.C. § 2612] to report periodically to the employer on the status and intention of the employee to return to work.

(b) Exemption concerning certain highly compensated employees. (1) Denial of restoration. An employer may deny restoration under subsection (a) to any eligible employee described in paragraph (2) if-

(A) such denial is necessary to prevent substantial and grievous economic injury to the operations of the employer;

(B) the employer notifies the employee of the intent of the employer to deny restoration on such basis at the time the employer determines that such injury would occur; and

(C) in any case in which the leave has commenced, the employee elects not to return to employment after receiving such notice.

(2) Affected employees. An eligible employee described in paragraph (1) is a salaried eligible employee who is among the highest paid 10 percent of the employ-

ees employed by the employer within 75 miles of the facility at which the employee is employed.

(c) Maintenance of health benefits. (1) Coverage. Except as provided in paragraph (2), during any period that an eligible employee takes leave under section 102 [29 U.S.C. § 2612], the employer shall maintain coverage under any "group health plan" (as defined in section 5000(b)(1) of the Internal Revenue Code of 1986 [26 U.S.C. § 5000(b)(1)]) for the duration of such leave at the level and under the conditions coverage would have been provided if the employee had continued in employment continuously for the duration of such leave.

(2) Failure to return from leave. The employer may recover the premium that the employer paid for maintaining coverage for the employee under such group health plan during any period of unpaid leave under section 102 [29 U.S.C. § 2612] if-

(A) the employee fails to return from leave under section 102 [29 U.S.C. § 2612] after the period of leave to which the employee is entitled has expired; and

(B) the employee fails to return to work for a reason other than-

(i) the continuation, recurrence, or onset of a serious health condition that entitles the employee to leave under subparagraph (C) or (D) of section 102(a)(1) [29 U.S.C. § 2612(a)(1); or

(ii) other circumstances beyond the control of the employee.

(3) Certification. (A) Issuance. An employer may require that a claim that an employee is unable to return

to work because of the continuation, recurrence, or onset of the serious health condition described in paragraph (2)(B)(i) be supported by-

(i) a certification issued by the health care provider of the son, daughter, spouse, or parent of the employee, as appropriate, in the case of an employee unable to return to work because of a condition specified in section 102(a)(1)(C) [29 U.S.C. § 2612(a)(1)(C)]; or

(ii) a certification issued by the health care provider of the eligible employee, in the case of an employee unable to return to work because of a condition specified in section 102(a)(1)(D) [29 U.S.C. § 2612(a)(1)(D)].

(B) Copy. The employee shall provide, in a timely manner, a copy of such certification to the employer.

(C) Sufficiency of certification. (i) Leave due to serious health condition of employee. The certification described in subparagraph (A)(ii) shall be sufficient if the certification states that a serious health condition prevented the employee from being able to perform the functions of the position of the employee on the date that the leave of the employee expired.

(ii) Leave due to serious health condition of family member. The certification described in subparagraph (A)(i) shall be sufficient if the certification states that the employee is needed to care for the son, daughter, spouse, or parent who has a serious health condition on the date that the leave of the employee expired.

§ 2615. Prohibited acts

(a) Interference with rights. (1) Exercise of rights. It shall be unlawful for any employer to interfere with, restrain, or deny the exercise of or the attempt to exercise, any right provided under this title [29 U.S.C. §§ 2611 et seq.].

(2) Discrimination. It shall be unlawful for any employer to discharge or in any other manner discriminate against any individual for opposing any practice made unlawful by this title [29 U.S.C. §§ 2611 et seq.].

(b) Interference with proceedings or inquiries. It shall be unlawful for any person to discharge or in any other manner discriminate against any individual because such individual-

(1) has filed any charge, or has instituted or caused to be instituted any proceeding, under or related to this title [29 U.S.C. §§ 2611 et seq.];

(2) has given, or is about to give, any information in connection with any inquiry or proceeding relating to any right provided under this title [29 U.S.C. §§ 2611 et seq.]; or

(3) has testified, or is about to testify, in any inquiry or proceeding relating to any right provided under this title [29 U.S.C. §§ 2611 et.seq.].

§ 2616. Investigative authority

(a) In general. To ensure compliance with the provisions of this title [29 U.S.C. §§ 2611 et seq.], or any regulation or order issued under this title [29 U.S.C. §§ 2611 et seq.), the Secretary shall have, subject to subsection (c), the investigative authority provided under section 11(a) of the Fair Labor Standards Act of 1938 (29 U.S.C. 211(a)).

(b) Obligation to keep and preserve records. Any employer shall make, keep, and preserve records pertaining to compliance with this title [29 U.S.C. §§ 2611 et.seq.] in accordance with section 11(c) of the Fair Labor Standards Act of 1938 (29 U.S.C. 211(c)) and in accordance with regulations issued by the Secretary.

(c) Required submissions generally limited to an annual basis. The Secretary shall not under the authority of this section require any employer or any plan, fund, or program to submit to the Secretary any books or records more than once during any 12-month period, unless the Secretary has reasonable cause to believe there may exist a violation of this title [29 U.S.C. §§ 2611 et seq.] or any regulation or order issued pursuant to this title [29 U.S.C. §§ 2611 et seq.], or is investigating a charge pursuant to section 107(b) [29 U.S.C. § 2617(b)].

(d) Subpoena powers. For the purposes of any investigation provided for in this section, the Secretary shall have the subpoena authority provided for under section 9 of the Fair Labor Standards Act of 1938 (29 U.S.C. 209).

§ 2617. Enforcement

(a) Civil action by employees. (1) Liability. Any employer who violates section 105 [29 U.S.C. §§ 2615] shall be liable to any eligible employee affected-

(A) for damages equal to-

(i) the amount of-

(I) any wages, salary, employment benefits, or other compensation denied or lost to such employee by reason of the violation; or

(II) in a case in which wages, salary, employment benefits, or other compensation have not been denied or lost to the employee, any actual monetary losses sustained by the employee as a direct
result of the violation, such as the cost of providing care, up to a sum equal to 12 weeks of wages or salary for the employee;

(ii) the interest on the amount described in clause (i) calculated at the prevailing rate; and

(iii) an additional amount as liquidated damages equal to the sum of the amount described in clause (i) and the interest described in clause (ii), except that if an employer who has violated section 105 [29 U.S.C. § 2615] proves to the satisfaction of the court that the act or omission which violated section 105 [29 U.S.C. § 2615] was in good faith and that the employer had reasonable grounds for believing that the act or omission was not a violation of section 105 (29 U.S.C. § 2615], such court may, in the discretion of the court, reduce the amount of the liability to the amount and interest determined under clauses (i) and (ii), respectively; and

(B) for such equitable relief as may be appropriate, including employment, reinstatement, and promotion.

(2) Right of action. An action to recover the damages or equitable relief prescribed in paragraph (1) may be

maintained against any employer (including a public agency) in any Federal or State court of competent jurisdiction by any one or more employees for and in behalf of-

(A) the employees; or

(B) the employees and other employees similarly situated.

(3) Fees and costs. The court in such an action shall, in addition to any judgment awarded to the plaintiff, allow a reasonable attorney's fee, reasonable expert witness fees, and other costs of the action to be paid by the defendant.

(4) Limitations. The right provided by paragraph (2) to bring an action by or on behalf of any employee shall terminate-

(A) on the filing of a complaint by the Secretary in an action under subsection (d) in which restraint is sought of any further delay in the payment of the amount described in paragraph (1)(A) to such employee by an employer responsible under paragraph (1) for the payment; or

(B) on the filing of a complaint by the Secretary in an action under subsection (b) in which a recovery is sought of the damages described in paragraph (1)(A) owing to an eligible employee by an employer liable under paragraph (1), unless the action described in subparagraph (A) or (B) is dismissed without prejudice on motion of the Secretary.

(b) Action by the Secretary. (1) Administrative action. The Secretary shall receive, investigate, and attempt to resolve complaints of violations of section 105 in the same manner that the Secretary receives, investigates, and attempts to resolve complaints of violations of sections 6 and 7 of the Fair Labor Standards Act of 1988 (29 U.S.C. §§ 206 and 207).

(2) Civil action. The Secretary may bring an action in any court of competent jurisdiction to recover the damages described in subsection (a)(1)(A).

(3) Sums recovered. Any sums recovered by the Secretary pursuant to paragraph (2) shall be held in a special deposit account and shall be paid, on order of the Secretary, directly to each employee affected. Any such sums not paid to an employee because of inability to do so within a period of 3 years shall be deposited into the Treasury of the United States as miscellaneous receipts.

(c) Limitation. (1) In general. Except as provided in paragraph (2), an action may be brought under this section not later than 2 years after the date of the last event constituting the alleged violation for which the action is brought.

(2) Willful violation. In the case of such action brought for a wailful violation of section 105 [29 U.S.C. § 2615], such action may be brought within 3 years of the date of the last event constituting the alleged violation for which such action is brought.

(3) Commencement. In determining when an action is commenced by the Secretary under this section for the purposes of this subsection, it shall be considered to be commenced on the date when the complaint is filed.

(d) Action for injunction by Secretary. The district courts of the United States shall have jurisdiction, for cause shown, in an action brought by the Secretary-

(1) to restrain violations of section 105 [29 U.S.C. §

2615], including the restraint of any withholding of payment of wages, salary, employment benefits, or other compensation, plus interest, found by the court to be due to eligible employees; or

(2) to award such other equitable relief as may be appropriate, including employment, reinstatement, and promotion.

(e) Solicitor of Labor. The Solicitor of Labor may appear for and represent the Secretary on any litigation brought under this section.

§ 2618. Special rules concerning employees of local educational agencies

(a) Application. (1) In general. Except as otherwise provided in this section, the rights (including the rights under section 104 [29 U.S.C. § 2614], which shall extend throughout the period of leave of any employee under this section), remedies, and procedures under this title [29 U.S.C. §§ 2611 et seq.] shall apply to-

(A) any "local educational agency" (as defined in section 1471(12) of the Elementary and Secondary Education Act of 1965 (20 U.S.C. 2891(12)) and an eligible employee of the agency; and

(B) any private elementary or secondary school and an eligible employee of the school.

(2) Definitions. For purposes of the application described in paragraph (1):

(A) Eligible employee. The term "eligible employee" means an eligible employee of an agency or school described in paragraph (1).

(B) Employer. The term "employer" means an agency or school described in paragraph (1).

(b) Leave does not violate certain other Federal laws. A local educational agency and a private elementary or secondary school shall not be in violation of the Individuals with Disabilities Education Act (20 U.S.C. §§ 1400 et seq.), section 504 of the Rehabilitation Act of 1973 (29 U.S.C. § 794), or title VI of the Civil Rights Act of 1964 (42 U.S.C. §§ 2000d et seq.), solely as a result of an eligible employee of such agency or school exercising the rights of such employee under this title [29 U.S.C. §§ 2611 et seq.].

(c) Intermittent leave or leave on a reduced schedule for instructional employees. (1) In general. Subject to paragraph (2), in any case in which an eligible employee employed principally in an instructional capacity by any such educational agency or school requests leave under subparagraph (C) or (D) of section 102(a)(1) [29 U.S.C. § 2612(a)(1)(C) or (D)] that is foreseeable based on planned medical treatment and the employee would be on leave for greater than 20 percent of the total number of working days in the period during which the leave would extend, the agency or school may require that such employee elect either-

(A) to take leave for periods of a particular duration, not to exceed the duration of the planned medical treatment; or

(B) to transfer temporarily to an available alternative position offered by the employer for which the employee is qualified, and that-

(i) has equivalent pay and benefits; and

(ii) better accommodates recurring periods of leave than the regular employment position of the employee.

(2) Application. The elections described in subparagraphs (A) and (B) of paragraph (1) shall apply only with respect to an eligible employee who complies with section 102(e)(2) [29 U.S.C. § 2612(e)(2)].

(d) Rules applicable to periods near the conclusion of an academic term. The following rules shall apply with respect to periods of leave near the conclusion of an academic term in the case of any eligible employee employed principally in an instructional capacity by any such educational agency or school:

(1) Leave more than 5 weeks prior to end of term. If the eligible employee begins leave under section 102 [29 U.S.C. § 2612] more than 5 weeks prior to the end of the academic term, the agency or school may require the employee to continue taking leave until the end of such term, if-

(A) the leave is of at least 3 weeks duration; and

(B) the return to employment would occur during the 3-week period before the end of such term.

(2) Leave less than 5 weeks prior to end of term. If the eligible employee begins leave under subparagraph (A), (B), or (C) of section 102(a)(1) [29 U.S.C. § 2612(a)(1)(A), (B), or (C)] during the period that commences 5 weeks prior to the end of the academic term, the agency or school may require the employee to continue taking leave until the end of such term, if-

(A) the leave is of greater than 2 weeks duration; and

(B) the return to employment would occur during the 2-week period before the end of such term.

(3) Leave less than 3 weeks prior to end of term. If the eligible employee begins leave under subparagraph (A), (B), or (C) of section 102(a)(1) [29 U.S.C. § 2612(a)(1)(A), (B), or (C)] during the period that commences 3 weeks prior to the end of the academic term and the duration of the leave is greater than 5 working days, the agency or school may require the employee to continue to take leave until the end of such term.

(e) Restoration to equivalent employment position. For purposes of determinations under section 104(a)(1)(B) [29 U.S.C. § 2614(a)(1)(B)] (relating to the restoration of an eligible employee to an equivalent position), in the case of a local educational agency or a private elementary or secondary school, such determination shall be made on the basis of established school board policies and practices, private school policies and practices, and collective bargaining agreements.

(f) Reduction of the amount of liability. If a local educational agency or a private elementary or secondary school that has violated this title [29 U.S.C. §§ 2611 et seq.] proves to the satisfaction of the court that the agency, school, or department had reasonable grounds for believing that the underlying act or omission was not a violation of this title 29 U.S.C. §§ 2611 et. seq.], such court may, in the discretion of the court, reduce the amount of the liability provided for under section 107(a)(1)(A) [29 U.S.C. § 2617(a)(1)(A)] to the amount and interest determined under clauses (i) and (ii), respectively, of such section.

§ 2619. Notice

(a) In general. Each employer shall post and keep posted, in conspicuous places on the premises of the employer where notices to employees and applicants for employment are customarily posted, a notice, to be prepared or approved by the Secretary, setting forth excerpts from, or summaries of, the pertinent provisions of this title [29 U.S.C. §§ 2611 et seq.] and information pertaining to the filing of a charge.

(b) Penalty. Any employer that willfully violates this section may be assessed a civil money penalty not to exceed $100 for each separate offense.

COMMISSION ON LEAVE

§ 2631. Establishment

There is established a commission to be known as the Commission on Leave (referred to in this title [29 U.S.C. §§ 2631 et seq.] as the "Commission").

§ 2632. Duties

The Commission shall-
(1) conduct a comprehensive study of-
(A) existing and proposed mandatory and voluntary policies relating to family and temporary medical leave, including policies provided by employers not covered under this Act;

(B) the potential costs, benefits, and impact on productivity, job creation and business growth of such policies on employers and employees;

(C) possible differences in costs, benefits, and impact on productivity, job creation and business growth of such policies on employers based on business type and size;

(D) the impact of family and medical leave policies on the availability of employee benefits provided by employers, including employers not covered under this Act;

(E) alternate and equivalent State enforcement of title I with respect to employees described in section 108(a) [29 U.S.C. § 2618(a)];

(F) methods used by employers to reduce administrative costs of implementing family and medical leave policies;

(G) the ability of the employers to recover, under section 104(c)(2) [29 U.S.C. § 2614(c)(2)], the premiums described in such section; and

(H) the impact on employers and employees of policies that provide temporary wage replacement during periods of family and medical leave.

(2) not later than 2 years after the date on which the Commission first meets, prepare and submit, to the appropriate Committees of Congress, a report concerning the subjects listed in paragraph (1).

§ 2633. Membership

(a) **Composition.** (1) Appointments. The Commission shall be composed of 12 voting members and 4 ex officio members to be appointed not later than 60 days after the date of the enactment of this Act [enacted Feb. 5, 1993 as follows:

(A) Senators. One Senator shall be appointed by the Majority Leader of the Senate, and one Senator shall be appointed by the Minority Leader of the Senate.

(B) Members of house of representatives. One Member of the House of Representatives shall be appointed by the Speaker of the House of Representatives, and one Member of the House of Representatives shall be appointed by the Minority Leader of the House of Representatives.

(C) Additional members. (i) Appointment. Two members each shall be appointed by-

(I) the Speaker of the House of Representatives;

(II) the Majority Leader of the Senate;

(III) the Minority Leader of the House of Representatives; and

(IV) the Minority Leader of the Senate.

(ii) Expertise. Such members shall be appointed by virtue of demonstrated expertise in relevant family, temporary disability, and labor management issues. Such members shall include representatives of employers, including employers from large businesses and from small businesses.

(2) Ex officio members. The Secretary of Health and Human Services, the Secretary of Labor, the Secretary of Commerce, and the Administrator of the Small Business Administration shall serve on the Commission as nonvoting ex officio members.

(b) Vacancies. Any vacancy on the Commission shall be filled in the manner in which the original appointment was made. The vacancy shall not affect the power of the remaining members to execute the duties of the Commission.

(c) Chair person and vice chair person. The Commission shall elect a chairperson and a vice chairperson from among the members of the Commission.

(d) Quorum. Eight members of the Commission shall constitute a quorum for all purposes, except that a lesser number may constitute a quorum for the purpose of holding hearings.

§ 2634. Compensation

(a) Pay. Members of the Commission shall serve without compensation.

(b) Travel expenses. Members of the Commission shall be allowed reasonable travel expenses, including a per diem allowance, in accordance with section 5703 of title 5, United States Code, when performing duties of the Commission.

§ 2635. Powers

(a) Meetings. The Commission shall first meet not later than 30 days after the date on which all members are appointed, and the Commission shall meet thereafter on the call of the chairperson or a majority of the members.

(b) Hearings and sessions. The Commission may hold such hearings, sit and act at such times and places, take such testimony, and receive such evidence as the Commission considers appropriate. The Commission may administer oaths or affirmations to witnesses appearing before it.

(c) Access to information. The Commission may secure directly from any Federal agency information necessary to enable it to carry out this title, if the information may be disclosed under section 552 of title 5, United States Code. Subject to the previous sentence, on the request of the chairperson or vice chairperson of the Commission, the head of such agency shall furnish such information to the Commission.

(d) Use of facilities and services. Upon the request of the Commission, the head of any Federal agency may make available to the Commission any of the facilities and services of such agency.

(e) Personnel from other agencies. On the request of the Commission, the head of any Federal agency may detail any of the personnel of such agency to serve as an Executive Director of the Commission or assist the Commission in carrying out the duties of the Commission. Any detail shall not interrupt or otherwise affect the civil service status or privileges of the Federal employee.

(f) Voluntary service. Notwithstanding section 1342 of title 31, United States Code, the chairperson of the Commission may accept for the Commission voluntary services provided by a member of the Commission.

§ 2636. Termination

The Commission shall terminate 30 days after the date of the submission of the report of the Commission to Congress.

MISCELLANEOUS PROVISIONS

§ 2651. Effect on other laws

(a) Federal and State antidiscrimination laws. Nothing in this Act or any amendment made by this Act shall be construed to modify or affect any Federal or State law prohibiting discrimination on the basis of race, religion, color, national origin, sex, age, or disability.

(b) State and local laws. Nothing in this Act or any amendment made by this Act shall be construed to supersede any provision of any State or local law that provides greater family or medical leave rights than the rights established under this Act or any amendment made by this Act.

§ 2652. Effect on existing employment benefits

(a) More protective. Nothing in this Act or any amendment made by this Act shall be construed to diminish the obligation of an employer to comply with any collective bargaining agreement or any employment benefit program or plan that provides greater family or medical leave rights to employees than the rights established under this Act or any amendment made by this Act.

(b) Less protective. The rights established for employees under this Act or any amendment made by this Act shall not be diminished by any collective bargaining agreement or any employment benefit program or plan.

§ 2653. Encouragement of more generous leave policies

Nothing in this Act or any amendment made by this Act shall be construed to discourage employers from adopting or retaining leave policies more generous than any policies that comply with the requirements under this Act or any amendment made by this Act.

§ 2654. Regulations

The Secretary of Labor shall prescribe such regulations as are necessary to carry out title I and this title [29 U.S.C. §§ 2611 et seq., 2651 et seq.] not later than 120 days after the date of the enactment of this Act [enacted Feb. 5, 1993].

AMERICANS WITH DISABILITIES ACT

TITLE I-EMPLOYMENT

Sec. 101 Definitions.
Sec. 102 Discrimination.
Sec. 103 Defenses.
Sec. 104 Illegal use of drugs and alcohol.
Sec. 105 Posting notices.
Sec. 106 Regulations.
Sec. 107 Enforcement.
Sec. 108 Effective date.

Sec. 2. Findings and Purposes

(a) Findings

The Congress finds that:

(1) some 43,000,000 Americans have one or more physical or mental disabilities, and this number is increasing as the population as a whole is growing older;

(2) historically, society has tended to isolate and segregate individuals with disabilities, and despite some improvements, such
as forms of discrimination against individuals with disabilities continue to be a serious and pervasive social problem;

(3) discrimination against individuals with disabilities persists in such critical areas as employment, housing, public accommodations, education, transportation, communication, recreation, institutionalization, health services, voting, and access to public services;

(4) unlike individuals who have experienced discrimination on the basis of race, color, sex, national origin, religion, or age, individuals who have experienced discrimination on the basis of disability have often had no legal recourse to redress such discrimination;

(5) individuals with disabilities continually encounter various forms of discrimination, including outright intentional exclusion, the discriminatory effects of architectural, transportation, and communication barriers, over-protective rules and policies, failure to make modifications to existing facilities and practices, exclusionary qualification standards and criteria, segregation,

and relegation to lesser services, programs, activities, benefits, jobs, or other opportunities;

(6) census data, national polls, and other studies have documented that people with disabilities, as a group, occupy an inferior status in our society, and are severely disadvantaged socially, vocationally, economically, and educationally;

(7) individuals with disabilities are a discrete and insular minority who have been faced with restrictions and limitations, subjected to a history of purposeful unequal treatment, and relegated to a position of political powerlessness in our society, based on characteristics that are beyond the control of such individuals and resulting from stereotypical assumptions not truly indicative of the individual ability of such individuals to participate in, and contribute to, society;

(8) the Nation's proper goals regarding individuals with disabilities are to assure equality of opportunity, full participation, independent living, and economic self-sufficiency for such individuals; and

(9) the continuing existence of unfair and unnecessary discrimination and prejudice denies people with disabilities the opportunity to compete on an equal basis and to pursue those opportunities for which our free society is justifiably famous, and costs the United States billions of dollars in unnecessary expenses resulting from dependency and non-productivity.

(b) Purpose

It is the purpose of this Act:

(I) to provide a clear and comprehensive national mandate for the elimination of discrimination against individuals with disabilities;

(2) to provide clear, strong, consistent, enforceable standards addressing discrimination against individuals with disabilities;

(3) to ensure that the Federal Government plays a central role in enforcing the standards established in this Act on behalf of individuals with disabilities; and

(4) to invoke the sweep of congressional authority, including the power to enforce the fourteenth amendment and to regulate commerce, in order to address the major areas of discrimination faced day-to-day by people with disabilities.

Sec. 3. Definitions

As used in this Act:

(1) AuxIliary Aids and Services

The term "auxiliary aids and services" includes:

(A) qualified interpreters or other effective methods of making aurally delivered materials available to individuals with hearing impairments;

(B) qualified readers, taped texts, or other effective methods of making visually delivered materials available to individuals with visual impairments;

(C) acquisition of modification of equipment or

devices; and

(D) other similar services and actions.

(2) Disabillty

The term "disability" means, with respect to an individual:

(A) a physical or mental impairment that substantially limits one or more of the major life activities of such individual;

(B) a record of such an impairment; or

(C) being regarded as having such an impairment.

(3) State

The term "State" means each of the several States, the District of Columbia, the Commonwealth of Puerto Rico, Guam, American Samoa, the Virgin Islands, the Trust Territory of the Pacific Islands, and the Commonwealth of the Northern Mariana Islands.

TITLE I-EMPLOYMENT

Sec. 101. Definitions

As used in this title:

(1) Commission

The term "Commission" means the Equal Employment Opportunity Commission established by section 705 of the Civil Rights Act of 1964 (42 U.S.C. 2000e-4).

(2) Covered Entity

The term "covered entity" means an employer, employment agency, labor organization, or joint labor-management committee.

(3) Direct Threat

The term "direct threat" means a significant risk to the health or safety of others that cannot be eliminated by reasonable accommodation.

(4) Employee

The term "employee" means an individual employed by an employer.

(5) Employer

(A) In general

The term "employer" means a person engaged in an industry affecting commerce who has 15 or more employees for each working day in each of 20 or more calendar weeks in the current or preceding calendar year, and any agent of such person, except that, for two years following the effective date of this title, an employer means a person engaged in an industry affecting commerce who has 25 or more employees of each working day in each of 20 or more calendar weeks in the current or preceding year, and any agent of such person.

(B) Exceptions

The term "employer" does not include:

(i) the United States, a corporation wholly owned by the government of the United States, or an Indian tribe; or

(ii) a bona fide private membership club (other than a labor organization) that is exempt from taxation under section 501(c) of the Internal Revenue Code of 1986.

(6) Illegal Use of Drugs

(A) In general
The term "illegal use of drugs" means the use of drugs, the possession or distribution of which is unlawful under the Controlled Substances Act (21 U.S.C. 812). Such term does not include the use of a drugs taken under supervision by a licensed health care professional, or other uses authorized by the Controlled Substances Act or other provisions of Federal law.

(B) Drugs
The term "drug" means a controlled substance, as defined in schedules I through V of section 202 of the Controlled Substances Act.

(7) Person, Etc.
The terms "persons," "labor organization," "employment agency," "commerce," and "industry affecting commerce," shall have the same meaning given such terms in section 701 of the Civil Rights Act of 1964 (42 U.S.C. 2000e).

(8) Qualified Individual with a Disability

The term "qualified individual with a disability" means an individual with a disability who, with or without reasonable accommodation, can perform the essential functions of the employment position that such individual holds or desires. For the purposes of this title, consideration shall be given to the employer's judgment as to what functions of a job are essential, and if an employer has prepared a written description before advertising or interviewing applicants for the job, this description shall be considered evidence of the essential functions of the job.

(9) Reasonable Accommodation

The term "reasonable accommodation" may include:

(A) making existing facilities used by employees readily accessible to and usable by individuals with disabilities; and

(B) job restructuring, part-time or modified work schedules, reassignment to a vacant position, acquisition or modification of equipment or devices, appropriate adjustment or modifications of examinations, training materials or policies, the provision of qualified readers or interpreters, and other similar accommodations for individuals with disabilities.

(10) Undue Hardship

(A) In general

The term "undue hardship" means an action requiring significant difficulty or expense, when considered in light of the factors set forth in subparagraph (B).

(B) Factors to be considered
In determining whether an accommodation would impose an undue hardship on a covered entity, factors to be considered include:

(i) the nature and cost of the accommodation needed under this Act;

(ii) the overall financial resources of the facility or facilities involved in the provision of the reasonable accommodation: the number of persons employed at such facility; the effect on expenses and resources, or the impact otherwise of such accommodation upon the operation of the facility;

(iii) the overall financial resources of the covered entity; the overall size of the business of a covered entity with respect to the number of its employees; the number, type, and location of its facilities; and

(iv) the type of operation or operations of the covered entity, including the composition, structure, and functions of the workforce of such entity; the geographic separateness, administrative, or fiscal relationship of the facility or facilities in question to the covered entity.

Sec. 102. Discrimination

(a) General Rule
No covered entity shall discriminate against a qualified individual with a disability because of the disability

of such individual in regard to job application procedures: the hiring, advancement, or discharge of employees, employee compensation, job training, and other terms, conditions, and privileges of employment.

(b) Construction

As used in subsection (a), the term "discriminate" includes:

(1) limiting, segregating, or classifying a job applicant or employee in a way that adversely affects the opportunities or status of such applicant or employee because of the disability of such applicant or employee;

(2) participating in a contractual or other arrangement or relationship that has the effect of subjecting a covered entity's qualified applicant or employee with a disability to the discrimination prohibited by this title (such relationship includes a relationship with an employment or referral agency, labor union, an organization providing fringe benefits to an employee of the covered entity, or an organization providing training and apprenticeship programs);

(3) utilizing standards, criteria, or methods of administration-

(A) that have the effect of discrimination on the basis of disability;
or
(B) that perpetuate the discrimination of others who are subject to common administrative control;

(4) excluding or otherwise denying equal jobs or benefits to a qualified individual because of the known dis-

ability of an individual with whom the qualified individual is known to have a relationship or association;

(5)(a) not making reasonable accommodations to the known physical or mental limitations of an otherwise qualified individual with a disability who is an applicant or employee, unless such covered entity can demonstrate that the accommodation would impose an undue hardship on the operation of the business of such covered entity; or

(b) denying employment opportunities to a job applicant or employee who is an otherwise qualified individual with a disability, if such denial is based on the need of such covered entity to make reasonable accommodation to the physical or mental impairments of the employee or applicant;

(6) using qualification standards, employment tests or other selection criteria that screen out or tend to screen out an individual with a disability or a class of individuals with disabilities unless the standard, test or other selection criteria, as used by the covered entity, is shown to be job related for the position in question and is consistent with business necessity; and

(7) failing to select and administer tests concerning employment in the most effective manner to ensure that, when such test is administered to a job applicant or employee who has a disability that impairs sensory, manual, or speaking skills, such test results accurately reflect the skills, aptitude, or whatever other factor of such applicant or employee that such test purports to measure, rather than reflecting the impaired sensory, manual, or

speaking skills of such employee or applicant (except where such skills are the factors that the test purports to measure).

(c) Medical Examinations and Inquiries

(1) In General
The prohibition against discrimination as referred to in subsection (a) shall include medical examinations and inquiries.

(2) Preemployment

(A) Prohibited examination or inquiry
Except as provided in paragraph (3), a covered entity shall not conduct a medical examination or make inquiries of a job applicant as to whether such applicant is an individual with a disability or as to the nature or severity of such disability.

(B) Acceptable inquiry
A covered entity may make preemployment inquiries into the ability of an applicant to perform job-related functions.

(3) Employment Entrance Examination
A covered entity may require a medical examination after an offer of employment has been made to a job applicant and prior to the commencement of the employment duties of such applicant, and may condition an offer of

employment on the results of such examination, if:

(A) all entering employees are subjected to such an examination regardless of disability;

(B) information obtained regarding the medical condition or history of the applicant is collected and maintained on separate forms and in separate medical files and is treated as a confidential medical record, except that-

(i) supervisors and managers may be informed regarding necessary restrictions on the work or duties of the employee and necessary accommodations;

(ii) first aid and safety personnel may be informed, when appropriate, if the disability might require emergency treatment; and

(iii) government officials investigating compliance with this Act shall be provided relevant information on request; and

(C) the results of such examination are used only in accordance with this title.

(4) Examination and Inquiry

(A) Prohibited examinations and inquiries

A covered entity shall not require a medical examination and shall not make inquiries of an employee as to whether such employee is an individual with a disability or as to the nature or severity of the disability, unless such examination or inquiry is shown to be job-related and consistent with business necessity.

(B) Acceptable examinations and inquiries

A covered entity may conduct voluntary medical examinations, including voluntary medical histories, which are part of an employee health program available to employees at the work site. A covered entity may make inquiries into the ability of an employee to perform job-related functions.

(C) Requirement

Information obtained under subparagraph (B) regarding the medical condition or history of any employee are subject to the requirements of subparagraphs (B) and (C) of paragraph (3).

Sec. 103. Defenses

(a) In General

It may be a defense to a charge of discrimination under this Act that an alleged application of qualification standards, tests, or selection criteria that screen out or tend to screen out or otherwise deny a job or benefit to an individual with a disability has been shown to be job-related and consistent with business necessity, and such performance cannot be accomplished by reasonable accommodation, as required under this title.

(b) Qualification Standards

The term "qualification standards" may include a requirement that an individual shall not pose a direct threat to the health or safety of other individuals in the workplace.

(c) Religious Entities

(1) In General
This title shall not prohibit a religious corporation, association, educational institution, or society from giving preference in employment to individuals of a particular religion to perform work connected with the carrying on by such corporation, association, education institution, or society of its activities.

(2) Religious Tenets Requirement
Under this title, a religious organization may require that all applicants and employees conform to the religious tenets of such organization.

(d) List of Infectious and Communicable Diseases

(1) In General
The Secretary of Health and Human Services, not later than 6 months after the date of enactment of this Act, shall:

(A) review all infectious and communicable diseases which may be transmitted through handling the food supply;

(B) publish a list of infectious and communicable diseases which are transmitted through handling the food supply;

(C) publish the method by which such diseases are

transmitted; and

(D) widely disseminate such information regarding the list of diseases and their modes of transmissibility to the general public.

Such list shall be updated annually.

(2) Application

In any case in which an individual has an infectious or communicable disease that is transmitted to others through the handling of food, that is included on the list developed by the Secretary of Health and Human Services under paragraph (1), and which cannot be eliminated by reasonable accommodation, a covered entity may refuse to assign or continue to assign such individual to a job involving food handling.

(3) Construction

Nothing in this Act shall be construed to preempt, modify, or amend any State, county, or local law, ordinance, or regulation applicable to good handling which is designed to protect the public health from individuals who pose a significant risk to the health or safety of others, which cannot be eliminated by reasonable accommodation, pursuant to the list of infectious or communicable diseases and the modes of transmissibility published by the Secretary of Health and Human Services.

Sec. 104. Illegal Use of Drugs and Alcohol

(a) Qualified Individual with a Disability

For purposes of this title, the term "qualified individual with a disability" shall not include any employee or applicant who is currently engaging in the illegal use of drugs, when the covered entity acts on the basis of such use.

(b) Rules of Construction

Nothing in subsection (a) shall be construed to exclude as a qualified individual with a disability an individual who:

(1) has successfully completed a supervised drug rehabilitation program and is no longer engaging in the illegal use of drugs, or has otherwise been rehabilitated successfully and is no longer engaging in such use;

(2) is participating in a supervised rehabilitation program and is no longer engaging in such use; or

(3) is erroneously regarded as engaging in such use, but is not engaging in such use;

except that it shall not be a violation of this Act for a covered entity to adopt or administer reasonable policies or procedures, including but not limited to drug testing, designed to ensure that an individual described in paragraph (1) or (2) is no longer engaging in the illegal use of drugs.

(c) Authority of Covered Entity

A covered entity:

(1) may prohibit the illegal use of drugs and the use of alcohol at the workplace by all employees;

(2) may require that employees shall not be under the influence of alcohol or be engaging in the illegal use of drugs at the workplace;

(3) may require that employees behave in conformance with the requirements established under the Drug-Free Workplace Act of 1988 (41 U.S.C. 701 et seq.);

(4) may hold an employee who engages in the illegal use of drugs or who is an alcoholic to the same qualification standards for employment or job performance and behavior that such entity holds other employees, even if any unsatisfactory performance or behavior is related to the drug use or alcoholism of such employee; and

(5) may, with respect to Federal regulations regarding alcohol and the illegal use of drugs, require that-

(A) employees comply with the standards established in such regulations of the Department of Defense, if the employees of the covered entity are employed in an industry subject to such regulations, including complying with regulations (if any) that apply to employment in sensitive positions in such an industry, in the case of employees of the covered entity who are employed in such positions (as defined in the regulations of the Department of Defense);

(B) employees comply with the standards established in such regulations of the Nuclear Regulatory Commission, if the employees of the covered entity are employed in an industry subject to such regulations, including complying with regulations (if any) that apply to employment in sensitive positions in such an industry, in the case of employees of the covered entity who are employed in such positions (as defined in the regulations of the Nuclear Regulatory Commission); and

(C) employees comply with the standards established in such regulations of the Department of Transportation, if the employees of the covered entity are employed in a transportation industry subject to such regulations, including complying with such regulations (if any) that apply to employment in sensitive positions in such an industry, in the case of employees of the covered entity who are employed in such positions (as defined in the regulations of the Department of Transportation).

(d) Drug Testing

(I) In General

For purposes of this title, a test to determine the illegal use of drugs shall not be considered a medical examination.

(2) Construction

Nothing in this title shall be construed to encourage, prohibit, or authorize the conducting of drug testing for the illegal use of drugs by job applicants or employees or making employment decisions based on such test results.

(e) Transportation Employees

Nothing in this title shall be construed to encourage, prohibit, restrict or authorize the otherwise lawful exercise by entities subject to the jurisdiction of the Department of Transportation of authority to:

(1) test employees of such entities in, and applicants for, positions involving safety-sensitive duties for the illegal use of drugs and for on-duty impairment of alcohol; and

(2) remove such persons who test positive for illegal use of drugs and on-duty impairment by alcohol pursuant to paragraph (I) from safety-sensitive duties in implementing subsection (c).

Sec. 105. Posting Notices

Every employer, employment agency, labor organization, or joint labor-management committee covered under this title shall post notices in an accessible format to applicants, employees, and members describing the applicable provisions of this Act, in the
manner prescribed by section 711 of the Civil Rights Act of 1964 (42 U.S.C. 2000e-10).

Sec. 106. Regulations

Not later than 1 year after the date of enactment of this Act, the Commission shall issue regulations in an accessible format to carry out this title in accordance with subchapter II of chapter 5 of title 5, United States Code.

Sec. 107. Enforcement

(a) Powers, Remedies, and Procedures

The powers, remedies, and procedures set forth in sections 705, 706, 707, 709 and 710 of the Civil Rights Act of 1964 (42 U.S.C. 2000e-4, 2000e-5, 2000e-6, 2000e-8, 2000e-9) shall be the powers, remedies, and procedures this title provides to the Commission, to the Attorney General, or to any person alleging discrimination on the basis of disability in violation of any provision of this Act, or regulations promulgated under section 106, concerning employment.

(b) Coordination

The agencies with enforcement authority for actions which allege employment discrimination under this title and under the Rehabilitation Act of 1973 shall develop procedures to ensure that administrative complaints filed under this title and under the Rehabilitation Act of 1973 are dealt with in a manner that avoids duplication of effort and prevents imposition of inconsistent or conflicting standards for the same requirements under this title and the Rehabilitation Act of 1973. The Commission, the Attorney General, and the Office of Federal Contract Compliance Programs shall establish such coordinating mechanisms (similar to provisions contained in the joint regulations promulgated by the Commission and the Attorney General at part 42 of title 28 and part 1691 of title 29, Code of Federal Regulations, and the Memorandum of Understanding between the Commission and the Office of

Federal Contract Compliance Programs dated January 16, 1981 (46 Fed Reg. 7435, January 23, 1981)) in regulations implementing this title and Rehabilitation Act of 1973 not later than 18 months after the date of enactment of this Act.